70 TRADITIONAL RECIPES FROM A
COUNTRY FARMHOUSE

70 TRADITIONAL RECIPES FROM A
COUNTRY FARMHOUSE

HOME COOKING AT ITS BEST, WITH CLASSIC RECIPES SHOWN IN
MORE THAN 250 STEP-BY-STEP PHOTOGRAPHS

CONSULTANT EDITOR: **JUDITH SIMONS**

southwater

This edition is published by Southwater, an imprint of Anness Publishing Ltd, Hermes House,
88–89 Blackfriars Road, London SE1 8HA; tel. 020 7401 2077; fax 020 7633 9499

www.southwaterbooks.com; www.annesspublishing.com

If you like the images in this book and would like to investigate using them for publishing, promotions or advertising,
please visit our website www.practicalpictures.com for more information.

UK distributor: Book Trade Services; tel. 0116 2759086; fax 0116 2759090; uksales@booktradeservices.com; exportsales@booktradeservices.com
North American distributor: National Book Network; tel. 301 459 3366; fax 301 429 5746; www.nbnbooks.com
Australian distributor: Pan Macmillan Australia; tel. 1300 135 113; fax 1300 135 103; customer.service@macmillan.com.au
New Zealand distributor: David Bateman Ltd; tel. (09) 415 7664; fax (09) 415 8892

Publisher: Joanna Lorenz
Project Editors: Gaby Goldsack, Linda Doeser
Editor: Jenni Fleetwood
Recipe contributors: Carla Capalbo, Jacqueline Clark, Maxine Clark, Frances Cleary, Carole Clements, Stephanie Donaldson, Joanna Farrow, Christine France,
Christine Ingram, Judy Jackson, Patricia Lousada, Norma MacMillan, Katherine Richmond, Laura Washburn, Steven Wheeler, Elizabeth Wolf-Cohen
Photographers: Karl Adamson, Edward Allwright, James Duncan, John Freeman, Michelle Garrett, Amanda Heywood, Patrick McLeavey
Designer: Siân Keogh, Axis Design
Illustrator: Anna Koska

ETHICAL TRADING POLICY

Because of our ongoing ecological investment programme, you, as our customer, can have the pleasure and reassurance of knowing that a tree is being
cultivated on your behalf to naturally replace the materials used to make the book you are holding. For further information about this scheme,
go to www.annesspublishing.com/trees

A CIP catalogue record for this book is available from the British Library.

Previously published as *Country Farmhouse Kitchen*

NOTES

For all recipes, quantities are given in both metric and imperial measures and, where appropriate, in standard cups and spoons. Follow one set
of measures, but not a mixture, because they are not interchangeable.
Standard spoon and cup measures are level. 1 tsp = 5ml, 1 tbsp = 15ml, 1 cup = 250ml/8fl oz.
Australian standard tablespoons are 20ml. Australian readers should use 3 tsp in place of 1 tbsp for measuring small quantities.
American pints are 16fl oz/2 cups. American readers should use 20fl oz/2.5 cups in place of 1 pint when measuring liquids.
Electric oven temperatures in this book are for conventional ovens. When using a fan oven, the temperature will probably need to be reduced by about
10–20°C/20–40°F. Since ovens vary, you should check with your manufacturer's instruction book for guidance.
Medium (US large) eggs are used unless otherwise stated.
Main front cover image shows Steak and Kidney Pie – for recipe, see page 64.

PUBLISHER'S NOTE

Although the advice and information in this book are believed to be accurate and true at the time of going to press, neither the authors nor the publisher
can accept any legal responsibility or liability for any errors or omissions that may have been made nor for any inaccuracies nor for any loss, harm or injury
that comes about from following instructions or advice in this book.

CONTENTS

Introduction

Good cooking depends on the best-quality and freshest ingredients, so it is hardly surprising that some of the finest cooking in the world can be found in the traditional country farmhouse kitchen. Tomatoes still warm from the sun, carrots just pulled from the soil, freshly podded peas and herbs plucked from the kitchen garden have a unique and special flavour, texture and aroma. They taste best when cooked simply, without elaborate sauces and dressings that would smother their freshness and delicacy. Meals to satisfy the heartiest appetite are equally characteristic of the farmhouse kitchen. After all, a day spent ploughing frost-hardened fields, a night spent lambing or a sun-baked week of harvesting works up an appetite.

Besides using home-grown vegetables and herbs, the farmhouse cook makes full use of the natural riches of the countryside. Nuts and mushrooms can be gathered in the woods and sloes and rosehips can be picked from the hedgerows. Nothing is wasted. If there is an abundant fruit harvest, jams and jellies will stock the pantry shelves, and chutneys and pickles are made from many different vegetables to spice up the winter months.

The country cook makes the most of the fresh produce of each season and in this book you will find a mouth-watering collection of recipes inspired by the farmhouse kitchen — soups, pies, casseroles, stews, cakes, bread and preserves. All are packed with flavour and will bring the taste of the country into any home.

Making Meat Stock

As every farmhouse cook will tell you, good home-made stock is the secret of successful meat soups, stews, casseroles, gravies and sauces.

INGREDIENTS

1.75 kg / 4–4½ lb beef bones, such as shin, leg, neck and clod, or veal or lamb bones, cut in 6 cm / 2½ in pieces
2 onions, unpeeled, quartered
2 carrots, roughly chopped
2 celery sticks, with leaves if possible, roughly chopped
2 tomatoes, coarsely chopped

4 litres / 6½ pints / 16 cups water
a handful of parsley stalks
a few fresh thyme sprigs or ¾ teaspoon dried thyme
2 bay leaves
10 black peppercorns, lightly crushed

Makes about 2 litres / 3½ pints/ 18 cups

1

Preheat the oven to 230°C / 450°F / Gas Mark 8. Put the bones in a roasting tin or flameproof casserole and roast, turning occasionally, for 30 minutes or until they start to brown.

2

Add the vegetables and baste with the fat in the tin or casserole. Roast for a further 20–30 minutes or until the bones are well browned. Stir and baste occasionally.

3

Transfer the bones and vegetables to a stockpot. Spoon off the fat from the roasting tin or casserole, add a little water and bring to the boil, scraping in any residue. Pour this liquid into the stockpot.

4

Add the remaining water. Bring just to the boil, skimming frequently to remove any foam. Add the herbs and peppercorns.

5

Partly cover the pot and simmer the stock for 4–6 hours, topping up the liquid as necessary.

6

Strain the stock. Skim as much fat as possible from the surface. If possible, cool the stock and then chill it; the fat will set in a layer on the surface and can be removed easily.

Making Chicken Stock

Use turkey to make the stock, if you prefer.

INGREDIENTS

*1.2–1.4 kg / 2½–3 lb chicken wings,
backs and necks (chicken, turkey, etc)
2 onions, unpeeled, quartered
4 litres / 6½ pints / 16 cups water
2 carrots, roughly chopped
2 celery sticks, with leaves if possible,
roughly chopped
a small handful of fresh parsley
a few fresh thyme sprigs or ¾ teaspoon
dried thyme
1 or 2 bay leaves
10 black peppercorns, lightly crushed*

Makes about 2.5 litres / 4 pints / 10 cups

1

Put the chicken pieces and the onions in a
stockpot. Cook over a medium heat,
stirring occasionally, until lightly browned.
Stir in the water. Bring to the boil. Skim
the surface.

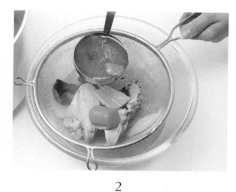

2

Add the remaining ingredients. Simmer for
3 hours. Strain, cool and chill. When cold,
remove the fat from the surface.

Making Vegetable Stock

Vary the ingredients for this fresh-flavoured stock according to what you have to hand.

INGREDIENTS

*2 large onions, coarsely chopped
2 leeks, sliced
3 garlic cloves, crushed
3 carrots, coarsely chopped
4 celery sticks, coarsely chopped
1 large strip of pared lemon rind
a handful of parsley stalks
a few fresh thyme sprigs
2 bay leaves
2.5 litres / 4 pints / 10 cups water*

Makes 2.5 litres / 4 pints / 10 cups

1

Put the vegetables, lemon rind, herbs and
water in a stockpot and bring to the boil.
Skim the surface.

2

Reduce the heat and simmer, uncovered, for
30 minutes. Strain the stock and leave it
to cool.

SOUPS &
STARTERS

Farmhouse Onion Soup

Slow, careful cooking is the secret of this traditional onion soup.

INGREDIENTS

*30 ml / 2 tbsp sunflower or olive oil,
or a mixture*
25 g / 1 oz / 2 tbsp butter
4 large onions, chopped
900 ml / 1½ pints / 3¾ cups beef stock
4 slices French bread
*40–50 g / 1½–2 oz Gruyère or
Cheddar cheese, grated*
salt and freshly ground black pepper

Serves 4

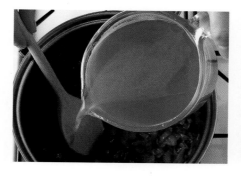

1

Heat the oil and butter in a deep saucepan and fry the onions briskly for 3–4 minutes. Reduce the heat and cook gently for 45–60 minutes.

2

When the onions are a rich mahogany brown, add the beef stock and a little seasoning. Simmer, partially covered, for 30 minutes, then taste and adjust the seasoning.

3

Preheat the grill and toast the French bread. Spoon the soup into four soup dishes that can safely be used under the grill. Place a piece of bread in each. Sprinkle with the cheese and grill for a few minutes until golden.

Country Vegetable Soup

This satisfying soup captures all the flavours of the countryside. The basil and garlic purée gives it extra colour and a wonderful aroma – so don't omit it.

INGREDIENTS

275 g / 10 oz / 1½ cups fresh shelled broad beans, or 175 g / 6 oz / ¾ cup dried haricot beans, soaked overnight in water to cover
2.5 ml / ½ tsp dried herbes de Provence
2 garlic cloves, finely chopped
15 ml / 1 tbsp olive oil
1 onion, finely chopped
2 small leeks, finely sliced
1 celery stick, finely sliced
2 carrots, finely diced
2 small potatoes, peeled and finely diced
115 g / 4 oz French beans
1.2 litres / 2 pints / 5 cups water
115 g / 4 oz / 1 cup peas, fresh or frozen
2 small courgettes, finely chopped
3 tomatoes, skinned, seeded and finely chopped
a handful of spinach leaves, cut into thin ribbons
salt and freshly ground black pepper
fresh basil sprigs, to garnish

For the garlic purée
1 or 2 garlic cloves, finely chopped
15 g / ½ oz / ½ cup basil leaves
60 ml / 4 tbsp grated Parmesan cheese
60 ml / 4 tbsp extra virgin olive oil

Serves 6–8

NOTE
To serve the soup, season and swirl a spoonful of purée into each bowl and garnish with basil.

1

To make the purée, process the garlic, basil and Parmesan until smooth. With the machine running, slowly add the olive oil through the feed-tube. Alternatively, put the garlic, basil and cheese in a mortar. Pound with a pestle, then stir in the oil.

3

Heat the oil in a saucepan. Fry the onion and leeks for 5 minutes, stirring occasionally.

5

Add the potatoes, French beans and water. Bring to the boil, then cover and simmer for 10 minutes.

2

If using dried beans, boil vigorously for 10 minutes and drain. Place them or fresh beans in a saucepan with the herbs and 1 garlic clove. Add water to cover by 2.5 cm / 1 in. Bring to the boil and simmer for 10 minutes for fresh beans or about 1 hour for dried beans.

4

Add the celery and carrots, with the remaining garlic clove. Cook for 10 minutes.

6

Add the peas, courgettes and tomatoes, with the reserved beans. Simmer for 25–30 minutes. Add the spinach, season to taste, and simmer for 5 minutes.

Summer Tomato Soup

The success of this soup depends on using ripe, full-flavoured tomatoes, such as the oval plum variety. It is traditionally made when the tomato season is at its peak.

INGREDIENTS

15 ml / 1 tbsp olive oil
1 large onion, chopped
1 carrot, chopped
1 kg / 2¼ lb ripe tomatoes, cored and quartered
2 garlic cloves, chopped
5 fresh thyme sprigs
4 or 5 fresh marjoram sprigs, plus extra for garnish
1 bay leaf
45 ml / 3 tbsp soured cream or yogurt, plus a little extra to garnish
salt and freshly ground black pepper

Serves 4

1

Heat the olive oil in a large saucepan. Cook the onion and carrot over a medium heat for 3–4 minutes until just softened, stirring occasionally.

2

Add the tomatoes, garlic and herbs. Simmer, covered, for 30 minutes, then sieve the soup into a clean pan. Stir in the soured cream or yogurt and season. Reheat gently and serve garnished with cream or yogurt and marjoram.

Pumpkin Soup

When the first frosts of autumn chill the air, bright orange pumpkins are a vivid sight in gardens and at country markets. Pumpkin soup is delicious.

INGREDIENTS

25 g / 1 oz / 2 tbsp butter
1 large onion, chopped
2 shallots, chopped
2 potatoes, peeled and cubed
900 g / 2 lb / 6 cups cubed pumpkin flesh
2 litres / 3½ pints / 8 cups chicken or vegetable stock
½ tsp ground cumin
pinch of freshly grated nutmeg
salt and freshly ground black pepper
fresh parsley or chives, to garnish

Serves 6–8

1

Melt the butter in a large saucepan and cook the onion and shallots for 4–5 minutes until just softened. Add the potatoes, pumpkin, stock and spices, with a little salt and black pepper. Simmer, covered, for about 1 hour, stirring occasionally.

2

With a slotted spoon, transfer the cooked vegetables to a food processor. Process until smooth, adding a little of the cooking liquid if needed. Stir the purée into the cooking liquid remaining in the pan. Adjust the seasoning and reheat gently. Serve garnished with the fresh herbs.

Stuffed Garlic Mushrooms

Flavoursome field mushrooms make a simply delicious starter when stuffed and baked.

INGREDIENTS

1 onion, chopped
75 g / 3 oz / 6 tbsp butter
8 field mushrooms of similar size
15 g / ½ oz / ¼ cup dried mushrooms,
soaked in warm water for 20 minutes
1 garlic clove, crushed
75 g / 3 oz / 1½ cups fresh
breadcrumbs
1 egg
75 ml / 5 tbsp chopped fresh parsley
15 ml / 1 tbsp chopped fresh thyme
115 g / 4 oz prosciutto, thinly sliced
salt and freshly ground black pepper
fresh parsley, to garnish

Serves 4

1

Preheat the oven to 190°C / 375°F / Gas Mark 5. Fry the onion gently in half the butter until soft. Break off the stems of the field mushrooms, setting the caps aside. Drain the dried mushrooms and chop these and the mushroom stems finely. Add to the onion, with the garlic, and cook for 2–3 minutes more.

2

Tip the mixture into a bowl and add the breadcrumbs, egg, herbs and seasoning. Melt the remaining butter and brush it over the mushroom caps. Arrange them on a baking sheet and spoon in the filling. Bake for 20–30 minutes until well browned. Top each mushroom with a strip of prosciutto, garnish with parsley and serve.

Mushroom Salad with Parma Ham

Ribbons of ham and pancake, tossed with wild mushrooms and salad leaves,
provide a feast for the eyes and the palate.

INGREDIENTS

40 g / 1½ oz / 3 tbsp butter, plus extra
for greasing
450 g / 1 lb assorted wild and
cultivated mushrooms, sliced
60 ml / 4 tbsp sherry
juice of ½ lemon
mixed lettuce leaves
30 ml / 2 tbsp walnut oil
175 g / 6 oz Parma ham, cut into ribbons

For the pancake ribbons
25 g / 1 oz / ¼ cup plain flour
75 ml / 5 tbsp milk
1 egg
60 ml / 4 tbsp grated Parmesan cheese
60 ml / 4 tbsp chopped fresh herbs
salt and freshly ground black pepper

Serves 4

1

To make the pancake, mix the flour and milk in a bowl. Beat in the egg, cheese, herbs and seasoning. Pour enough of the mixture into a hot, greased frying pan to coat the bottom of it. When set, turn the pancake over and cook briefly on the other side. Cool, then roll up and slice into ribbons. Repeat with the remaining batter.

2

Cook the mushrooms in the butter for 6–8 minutes. Add the sherry and lemon juice, and season to taste.

3

Toss the lettuce in the oil and arrange on four plates. Place the ham and pancake ribbons in the centre and spoon on the mushrooms.

Country-style Pâté with Leeks

A rough pâté is very much a feature of the farmhouse kitchen. Cooked slowly so that all the flavours combine, then pressed, it makes a perfect starter or light lunch.

15 g / ½ oz / 1 tbsp butter
450 g / 1 lb leeks (white and pale green parts), sliced
2 or 3 large garlic cloves, finely chopped
1 kg / 2¼ lb lean pork leg or shoulder, trimmed and cubed
150 g / 5 oz rindless smoked streaky bacon rashers
7.5 ml / 1½ tsp chopped fresh thyme
3 fresh sage leaves, finely chopped
¼ tsp quatre épices (mixed ground cloves, cinnamon, nutmeg and black pepper)
¼ tsp ground cumin
pinch of freshly grated nutmeg
½ tsp salt
5 ml / 1 tsp freshly ground black pepper
1 bay leaf

Serves 8–10

1

Melt the butter in a large, heavy-based frying pan, add the leeks, then cover and sweat over a low heat for 10 minutes, stirring occasionally. Add the garlic and continue cooking for about 10 minutes until the leeks are very soft, then set aside to cool.

2

Pulse the meat cubes in batches in a food processor to chop it coarsely. Alternatively, pass the meat through the coarse blade of a mincer. Transfer the meat to a large mixing bowl and remove any white stringy bits. Reserve two of the bacon rashers for garnishing, then chop or grind the remainder, and mix with the pork in the mixing bowl.

3

Preheat the oven to 180°C / 350°F / Gas Mark 4. Line the base and sides of a 1.5 litre / 2½ pint / 6 cup terrine with greaseproof paper or baking parchment. Add the leek mixture, herbs and spices to the pork mixture, with the salt and pepper.

4

Spoon the mixture into the terrine, pressing it into the corners and compacting it. Tap firmly to settle the mixture and smooth the top. Arrange the bay leaf and bacon rashers on top, then cover tightly with foil.

5

Place the terrine in a roasting tin and pour in boiling water to come halfway up the side. Bake for 1¼ hours. Drain off the water, then return the terrine to the roasting tin and place a baking sheet on top. Weight with two or three large cans or a foil-wrapped clean house brick while the pâté cools. Chill overnight, before slicing.

VEGETABLES

Leeks in Egg and Lemon Sauce

*Tender young leeks, picked fresh from the vegetable plot, cooked and cooled
in a tart creamy sauce, taste absolutely superb.*

INGREDIENTS

*675 g / 1½ lb baby leeks, trimmed,
slit and washed
15 ml / 1 tbsp cornflour
10 ml / 2 tsp sugar
2 egg yolks
juice of 1½ lemons
salt*

Serves 4

3

Whisk the egg yolks with the lemon juice
and stir gradually into the cooled sauce.
Cook over a very low heat, stirring all the
time, until the sauce is fairly thick.
Immediately remove from the heat and
continue stirring for 1 minute. Taste and
add salt or sugar as necessary. Cool slightly.

4

Pour the sauce over the leeks. Cover and
chill for at least 2 hours before serving.

NOTE
Do not let the sauce overheat after adding
the egg yolks or it may curdle.

1

Lay the leeks flat in a large saucepan, cover
with water and add a little salt. Bring to
the boil, lower the heat, cover and simmer
for 4–5 minutes until just tender.

2

Lift out the leeks, drain well and arrange in
a shallow serving dish. Mix 200 ml / 7 fl
oz / scant 1 cup of the cooking liquid with
the cornflour in a saucepan. Bring to the
boil, stirring all the time, then cook until
the sauce thickens slightly. Stir in the
sugar. Cool slightly.

Braised Red Cabbage

The combination of red wine vinegar and sugar gives this dish a sweet yet tart flavour.
In France it is often served with game, but it is also delicious with pork, duck or cold meats.

INGREDIENTS

30 ml / 2 tbsp vegetable oil
2 onions, thinly sliced
2 eating apples, peeled, cored and thinly sliced
1 head red cabbage (about 900 g / 2 lb), trimmed, cored, halved and thinly sliced
60 ml / 4 tbsp red wine vinegar
15–30 ml / 1–2 tbsp granulated sugar
¼ tsp ground cloves
5–10 ml / 1–2 tsp mustard seeds
50 g / 2 oz / ⅓ cup raisins or currants
about 120 ml / 4 fl oz / ½ cup red wine or water
15–30 ml / 1–2 tbsp redcurrant jelly
salt and freshly ground black pepper

Serves 6–8

1

Heat the oil in a large, stainless steel saucepan over a medium heat. Fry the onions for 7–10 minutes until golden. Stir in the apples and cook, stirring, for 2–3 minutes, until just softened.

2

Add the cabbage, red wine vinegar, sugar, cloves, mustard seeds, raisins or currants, red wine or water, and salt and pepper, stirring until well mixed. Bring to the boil, stirring occasionally.

3

Cover and cook over a fairly low heat for 35–40 minutes until the cabbage is tender and the liquid is just absorbed, stirring occasionally. Add a little more red wine or water if the pan boils dry before the cabbage is tender. Just before serving, stir in the redcurrant jelly to sweeten and glaze the cabbage.

Salsify and Spinach Bake

The spinach in this recipe adds colour and makes it go further. However, if you have plenty of salsify, plus the patience to peel it, increase the quantity and leave out the spinach.

INGREDIENTS

juice of 2 lemons
450 g / 1 lb salsify
450 g / 1 lb fresh spinach leaves
150 ml / ¼ pint / ⅔ cup chicken or vegetable stock
300 ml / ½ pint / 1¼ cups single cream
salt and freshly ground black pepper

Serves 4

1

Preheat the oven to 160°C / 325°F / Gas Mark 3. Add a quarter of the lemon juice to a large bowl of water. Top, tail and peel the salsify. Place each peeled root immediately in the acidulated water, to prevent discoloration. Bring a saucepan of water to the boil. Add the remaining lemon juice. Cut the salsify into 5 cm / 2 in lengths, add it to the pan and simmer for about 10 minutes, until just tender.

2

Meanwhile, cook the spinach in a large saucepan over a medium heat for 2–3 minutes until the leaves have wilted, shaking the pan occasionally. Place the stock, cream and seasoning in a small saucepan and heat through very gently, stirring.

3

Grease a baking dish generously with butter. Drain the salsify and spinach and arrange in layers in the prepared dish. Pour over the stock and cream mixture and bake for about 1 hour until the top is golden brown and bubbling.

Rosemary Roasties

These unusual roast potatoes use far less fat than conventional roast potatoes, and because they still have their skins they have more flavour too.

INGREDIENTS

*1 kg / 2¼ lb red potatoes
10 ml / 2 tsp walnut or sunflower oil
30 ml / 2 tbsp fresh rosemary leaves
salt and paprika*

Serves 4

NOTE
This is also delicious with tiny salad potatoes, especially if you roast them with chunks of red onion.

1

Preheat the oven to 240°C / 475°F / Gas Mark 9. Scrub the potatoes. If they are large, cut them in half. Place in a pan of cold water and bring to the boil. Drain.

2

Drizzle the oil over the potatoes and shake the pan to coat them evenly.

3

Tip the potatoes into a shallow roasting tin. Sprinkle with the rosemary, salt and paprika. Roast for 30–45 minutes. Serve hot.

Baked Courgettes in Tomato Sauce

Courgettes and tomatoes have a natural affinity. Use fresh tomatoes, cooked and puréed, instead of passata if possible.

INGREDIENTS

*5 ml / 1 tsp olive oil
3 large courgettes, thinly sliced
½ small red onion, finely chopped
300 ml / ½ pint / 1¼ cups passata
(puréed tomatoes)
30 ml / 2 tbsp chopped fresh thyme
garlic salt and freshly ground black
pepper
fresh thyme sprigs, to garnish*

Serves 4

1

Preheat the oven to 190°C / 375°F / Gas Mark 5. Brush a baking dish with olive oil. Arrange half the courgettes and onion in the dish.

2

Spoon half the passata over the vegetables. Sprinkle with some of the fresh thyme, then season to taste with garlic salt and pepper. Repeat with the remaining ingredients. Cover the dish and bake for 40–45 minutes. Garnish with thyme sprigs and serve hot.

Spicy Fried Potatoes

Give fried potatoes a hint of heat by tossing them with spiced vinegar.
Sliced peppers add a splash of colour.

INGREDIENTS

2 garlic cloves, sliced
½ tsp crushed chillies
½ tsp ground cumin
10 ml / 2 tsp paprika
30 ml / 2 tbsp red or white wine
vinegar
675 g / 1½ lb small new potatoes
75 ml / 5 tbsp olive oil
1 red or green pepper, seeded and sliced
coarse sea salt, to serve (optional)

Serves 4

1

Mix the garlic, chillies and cumin in a mortar. Crush with a pestle, then stir in the paprika and wine vinegar.

2

Bring a saucepan of lightly salted water to the boil and cook the potatoes, in their skins, for about 15 minutes until almost tender. Drain, peel, if preferred, and cut into chunks. Heat the oil in a large frying pan; sauté the potatoes until golden.

3

Add the spiced garlic mixture to the potatoes with the sliced pepper and continue to cook, stirring, for 2 minutes. Serve warm, or leave until cold. Scatter with coarse sea salt, if you like, to serve.

Turnip Tops with Parmesan and Garlic

Farmhouse cooks know how to turn everyday ingredients into treats. Here, turnip tops are flavoured with onions, garlic and Parmesan cheese. They do not need long cooking as the leaves are quite tender.

INGREDIENTS

45 ml / 3 tbsp olive oil
2 garlic cloves, crushed
4 spring onions, sliced
350 g / 12 oz turnip tops, thinly sliced, tough stalks removed
60 ml / 4 tbsp water
50 g / 2 oz / ⅔ cup grated Parmesan cheese
salt and freshly ground black pepper
shavings of Parmesan cheese, to garnish

Serves 4

1

Heat the olive oil in a large saucepan and stir-fry the garlic and spring onions for 2 minutes. Add the turnip tops and stir-fry for 2–3 minutes so that the greens are coated in oil. Add the water.

2

Bring to the boil, lower the heat, cover and simmer, stirring frequently, until the greens are tender. Bring the liquid to the boil again, allow the excess to evaporate, then stir in the Parmesan and seasoning. Serve at once with extra shavings of cheese.

Glazed Carrots with Cider

Cooking young carrots with the minimum of liquid brings out the best of their flavour, and the cider adds a pleasant sharpness.

INGREDIENTS

450 g / 1 lb young carrots
25 g / 1 oz / 2 tbsp butter
15 ml / 1 tbsp soft brown sugar
120 ml / 4 fl oz / ½ cup cider
60 ml / 4 tbsp vegetable stock
5 ml / 1 tsp Dijon mustard
15 ml / 1 tbsp finely chopped fresh parsley

Serves 4

NOTE

If the carrots are cooked before the liquid in the frying pan has reduced, transfer the carrots to a serving dish and rapidly boil the liquid until thick. Pour the liquid over the carrots and sprinkle with parsley.

1

Trim the tops and bottoms of the carrots. Peel or scrape them. Using a sharp knife, cut them into matchstick strips. Melt the butter in a frying pan and sauté the carrots for 4–5 minutes.

2

Sprinkle over the sugar and cook, stirring, for 1 minute. Add the cider and stock, bring to the boil and stir in the mustard. Partially cover the pan and simmer for 10–12 minutes until the carrots are just tender. Remove the lid and continue cooking until the liquid has reduced to a thick sauce. Toss the carrots with the parsley and spoon into a warmed serving dish.

Carrot, Apple and Orange Coleslaw

This dish is as delicious as it is easy to make. The garlic and herb dressing adds the necessary contrast to the sweetness of the salad.

INGREDIENTS

350 g / 12 oz young carrots, finely grated
2 eating apples
15 ml / 1 tbsp lemon juice
1 large orange, peeled and segmented

For the dressing
45 ml / 3 tbsp olive oil
60 ml / 4 tbsp sunflower oil
45 ml / 3 tbsp lemon juice
1 garlic clove, crushed
60 ml / 4 tbsp natural yogurt
15 ml / 1 tbsp chopped mixed fresh herbs
salt and freshly ground black pepper

Serves 4

1

Place the carrots in a large serving bowl. Quarter the apples, remove the core from each wedge and then slice thinly. Sprinkle the apples with lemon juice to prevent discoloration, then add to the carrots, with the orange segments.

2

To make the dressing, place the oils, lemon juice and garlic in a jar with a tight-fitting lid and shake vigorously. Add the remaining ingredients and shake again. Just before serving, pour the dressing over the salad and toss well.

Brussels Sprouts with Chestnuts

A traditional Christmas speciality, this combination of crisp, tender Brussels sprouts and chestnuts is perennially popular.

INGREDIENTS

225 g / 8 oz chestnuts
120 ml / 4 fl oz / ½ cup milk
*500 g / 1¼ lb / 4 cups small tender
Brussels sprouts*
25 g / 1 oz / 2 tbsp butter
1 shallot, finely chopped
*30–45 ml / 2–3 tbsp dry white wine
or water*

Serves 4–6

1

Cut a cross in the base of each chestnut.
Bring a saucepan of water to the boil, drop
in the chestnuts and boil for 6–8 minutes.
Peel while still warm, then return to the
clean pan. Add the milk and enough water
to cover the chestnuts. Simmer for
12–15 minutes. Drain and set aside.

2

Remove any wilted or yellow leaves from
the Brussels sprouts. Trim the root end but
leave intact or the leaves will separate.
Using a small knife, cut a cross in the base
of each sprout.

3

Melt the butter in a large, heavy-based
frying pan, and cook the shallot for
1–2 minutes until just softened. Add the
Brussels sprouts and wine or water. Cover
and cook over a medium heat for
6–8 minutes, shaking the pan occasionally
and adding a little more water if necessary.

4

Add the poached chestnuts and toss gently,
then cover and cook for 3–5 minutes more.
Serve at once.

Leek Tart

This unusual recipe isn't a normal tart with pastry, but an all-in-one savoury slice that is excellent served as an accompaniment to roast meat.

INGREDIENTS

50 g / 2 oz / 4 tbsp unsalted butter
350 g / 12 oz leeks, sliced thinly
225 g / 8 oz / 2 cups self-raising flour
115 g / 4 oz / ½ cup grated hard white fat
150 ml / ¼ pint / ⅔ cup water
salt and freshly ground black pepper

Serves 4

1

Preheat the oven to 200°C / 400°F / Gas Mark 6. Melt the butter in a pan and sauté the leeks until soft. Season well.

2

Mix the flour, fat and water together in a bowl to make a soft but sticky dough. Mix into the leek mixture in the pan. Place in a greased shallow overproof dish and bake for 30 minutes, or until brown and crispy. Serve sliced, as a vegetable accompaniment.

Squash à la Greque

A traditional French-style dish that is usually made with mushrooms. Make sure you cook the squash until they are quite tender, so they absorb the delicious flavours of the marinade.

INGREDIENTS

175 g / 6 oz patty-pan squash
250 ml / 8 fl oz / 1 cup white wine
juice of 2 lemons
fresh thyme sprig
bay leaf
small bunch of fresh chervil,
roughly chopped
¼ tsp coriander seeds, crushed
¼ tsp black peppercorns, crushed
75 ml / 5 tbsp olive oil

Serves 4

1

Blanch the patty-pan squash in boiling water for 3 minutes, then refresh them with cold water.

2

Place all the remaining ingredients in a pan, add 150 ml / ½ pint / ⅔ cup water and simmer for 10 minutes, covered. Add the patty-pans and cook for 10 minutes. Remove with a slotted spoon when they are cooked and tender to the bite.

3

Reduce the liquid by boiling hard for 10 minutes. Strain it and pour it over the squashes. Leave until cool for the flavours to be absorbed. Serve cold.

Stuffed Parsleyed Onions

Although devised as a vegetarian dish, these stuffed onions make a wonderful accompaniment to meat dishes, or an appetizing supper dish with crusty bread and a salad.

INGREDIENTS

4 large onions
4 tbsp cooked rice
4 tsp finely chopped fresh parsley,
plus extra to garnish
4 tbsp strong Cheddar cheese,
finely grated
salt and pepper
2 tbsp olive oil
1 tbsp white wine, to moisten

Serves 4

1

Cut a slice from the top of each onion and scoop out the centre to leave a thick shell.

2

Combine all the remaining ingredients, moistening with enough wine to mix well. Preheat the oven to 180°C / 350°F / Gas Mark 4.

3

Fill the onions and bake in the oven for 45 minutes. Serve garnished with parsley.

EGGS & CHEESE

Eggs in Pepper Nests

Pepper strips look pretty and provide an interesting base for baked eggs topped with cream.

INGREDIENTS

2 red peppers
1 green pepper
30 ml / 2 tbsp olive oil
1 large onion, finely sliced
2 garlic cloves, crushed
5–6 tomatoes, skinned and chopped
120 ml / 4 fl oz / ½ cup passata or
tomato juice
good pinch of dried basil
4 eggs
40 ml / 8 tsp single cream
pinch of cayenne pepper (optional)
salt and freshly ground black pepper

Serves 4

1

Preheat the oven to 180°C / 350°F / Gas Mark 4. Seed and thinly slice the peppers. Heat the olive oil in a large frying pan. Fry the onion and garlic gently for about 5 minutes, stirring, until softened.

2

Add the peppers to the onion and fry for 10 minutes. Stir in the tomatoes and passata or juice, the basil and seasoning. Cook gently for 10 minutes more until the peppers are soft.

3

Spoon the mixture into four ovenproof dishes. Make a hole in the centre of each and break in an egg. Spoon 10 ml / 2 tsp cream over the yolk of each egg and sprinkle with a little black pepper or cayenne. Bake for 12–15 minutes until the white of the egg is lightly set. Serve at once with crusty bread.

Cheese and Bacon Quiche

Quiches are great country fare, ideal for al fresco meals. To pack for a picnic, double wrap the tin in foil and support it in a stout box.

INGREDIENTS

*350 g / 12 oz shortcrust pastry,
thawed if frozen
15 ml / 1 tbsp Dijon mustard
175 g / 6 oz / 6 rindless streaky
bacon rashers, chopped
3 eggs
350 ml / 12 fl oz / 1½ cups single cream
1 onion, chopped
150 g / 5 oz Gruyère cheese, diced
salt and freshly ground black pepper
fresh parsley, to garnish*

Serves 6–8

1

Preheat the oven to 200°C / 400°F / Gas Mark 6. Roll out the pastry and line a 23 cm / 9 in flan tin. Prick the base of the pastry case and bake for 15 minutes. Brush the case with mustard and bake for 5 minutes more. Reduce the oven temperature to 180°C / 350°F / Gas Mark 4.

2

Fry the bacon until crisp and browned. Beat the eggs and cream, season with salt and pepper and set aside.

3

Drain the bacon. Pour off most of the fat from the pan, add the onion and cook gently for about 15 minutes.

4

Sprinkle half the cheese over the pastry, then the onion, followed by the bacon and remaining cheese. Pour on the egg mixture and bake for 35–45 minutes until set. Serve warm, garnished with parsley.

Eggs Baked in Ham and Potato Hash

INGREDIENTS

50 g / 2 oz / ¼ cup butter
1 large onion, chopped
350 g / 12 oz cooked ham, diced
450 g / 1 lb cooked potatoes, diced
115 g / 4 oz / 1 cup grated Cheddar
cheese
30 ml / 2 tbsp tomato ketchup
30 ml / 2 tbsp Worcestershire sauce
6 eggs
few drops of Tabasco sauce
salt and freshly ground black pepper
chopped fresh chives, to garnish

Serves 6

3

Make six hollows in the hash. Break each egg in turn into a small bowl or saucer and slip into one of the hollows.

4

Melt the remaining butter. Season with Tabasco sauce, then dribble the seasoned butter over the eggs and hash. Bake for 15–20 minutes or until the eggs are set. Garnish with chives and serve.

1

Preheat the oven to 160°C / 325°F / Gas Mark 3. Melt half the butter in a frying pan. Cook the onion until soft, stirring occasionally, then tip it into a bowl and stir in the ham, potatoes, cheese, ketchup and Worcestershire sauce.

2

Season the mixture and spread it in a buttered baking dish in a layer about 2.5 cm / 1 in deep. Bake for 10 minutes.

Omelette with Herbs

Sometimes the simplest dishes are the most satisfying. Fresh farm eggs, lightly soured cream and herbs make a speedy but superb meal.

INGREDIENTS

2 eggs
15 g / ½ oz / 1 tbsp butter
15 ml / 1 tbsp crème fraîche or soured cream
5 ml / 1 tsp chopped fresh mixed herbs (such as tarragon, chives, parsley or marjoram)
salt and freshly ground black pepper

Serves 1

VARIATIONS
Other omelette fillings could include sautéed sliced mushrooms, diced ham or crumbled crisp bacon, creamed spinach or thick tomato sauce and grated cheese.

1
Beat the eggs and salt and pepper in a bowl. Melt the butter in an omelette pan until foamy, then pour in the eggs. When the mixture starts to set on the base of the pan, lift up the sides with a palette knife and tilt the pan to allow the uncooked egg to run underneath.

2
When the omelette is set, but still soft on top, spoon the crème fraîche or soured cream over the centre and sprinkle with the herbs. Hold the pan over a warmed plate. With a palette knife, lift one edge of the omelette and fold it over the middle. Tilt the pan so that the omelette folds in thirds and slide it out on to the plate.

Egg-stuffed Tomatoes

Effective, but surprisingly easy to prepare, this is the perfect dish for a quick lunch. For the most enjoyable result, eat immediately.

INGREDIENTS

175 ml / 6 fl oz / ¾ cup mayonnaise
30 ml / 2 tbsp snipped fresh chives
30 ml / 2 tbsp torn fresh basil leaves
30 ml / 2 tbsp chopped fresh parsley
4 ripe tomatoes
4 hard-boiled eggs, sliced
salt
lettuce leaves, to serve

Serves 4

1
Mix the mayonnaise and herbs in a small bowl and set aside. Place the tomatoes core-end down and make deep cuts to within 1 cm / ½ in of the base. (There should be the same number of cuts in each tomato as there are slices of egg.)

2
Fan open the tomatoes and sprinkle with salt, then insert an egg slice into each slit. Place each stuffed tomato on a plate with lettuce leaves and serve with the herb mayonnaise.

Cauliflower Cheese

An old favourite that never loses its popularity, this is equally good with broccoli. Serve it with grilled locally-cured bacon for a special treat.

INGREDIENTS

450 g / 1 lb cauliflower, broken into florets
40 g / 1½ oz / 3 tbsp butter
40 g / 1½ oz / 6 tbsp plain flour
350 ml / 12 fl oz / 1½ cups milk
1 bay leaf
pinch of grated nutmeg
15 ml / 1 tbsp Dijon mustard
175 g / 6 oz / 1½ cups grated Gruyère or Emmenthal cheese
salt and freshly ground black pepper

Serves 4–6

1

Preheat the oven to 180°C / 350°F / Gas Mark 4. Lightly butter a large gratin dish or shallow baking dish.

2

Bring a large saucepan of salted water to the boil, add the cauliflower florets and cook for 6–8 minutes until just tender.

3

Melt the butter in a heavy saucepan over a medium heat, add the flour and cook until just golden, stirring occasionally. Gradually add the milk, stirring constantly until the sauce boils and thickens. Add the bay leaf and salt, pepper and nutmeg. Add the mustard. Reduce the heat and simmer for 5 minutes, stirring occasionally, then remove the bay leaf. Stir in half the cheese.

4

Arrange the cauliflower in the dish. Pour over the cheese sauce and sprinkle with the remaining cheese. Bake for about 20 minutes until bubbly and well browned.

Poached Eggs with Spinach

When the vegetable garden yields fresh spinach, serve this simple dish.

INGREDIENTS

25 g / 1 oz / 2 tbsp butter
450 g / 1 lb young spinach leaves
½ tsp vinegar
4 eggs
salt and freshly ground black pepper

For the hollandaise sauce
2 egg yolks
15 ml / 1 tbsp lemon juice
15 ml / 1 tbsp water
175 g / 6 oz / ¾ cup butter, diced
salt and white pepper

Serves 4

NOTE
For a well-shaped poached egg, swirl the water whirlpool-fashion before slipping the egg into the centre.

1

Make the hollandaise sauce. Whizz the egg yolks, lemon juice and water in a food processor. Melt the butter in a small pan until foaming. With the machine running, slowly pour the hot butter into the processor in a thin stream. Season the thickened sauce with more lemon juice if needed and salt and pepper. Transfer the sauce to a bowl, cover and keep warm.

2

Melt the butter in a heavy-based frying pan over a medium heat. Add the spinach and cook until wilted, stirring occasionally. Season and keep warm.

3

Bring a pan of lightly salted water to the boil and add the vinegar. Break an egg into a saucer and slide the egg into the water. Reduce the heat and simmer for a few minutes until the white is set and the yolk is still soft. Remove with a slotted spoon and drain. Trim any untidy edges with scissors and keep the poached egg warm. Poach the remaining eggs in the same way.

4

To serve, spoon the spinach on to warmed plates and make a hollow in each mound. Place the eggs on top and pour over a little hollandaise sauce.

FISH & SEAFOOD

Chunky Seafood Stew

*There's no more pleasant way of spending an evening than sitting around the scrubbed
farmhouse table and tucking into an excellent seafood stew.*

INGREDIENTS

45 ml / 3 tbsp olive oil
2 large onions, chopped
1 small green pepper, seeded and sliced
3 carrots, chopped
3 garlic cloves, crushed
30 ml / 2 tbsp tomato purée
2 x 400 g / 14 oz cans chopped tomatoes
45 ml / 3 tbsp chopped fresh parsley
5 ml / 1 tsp chopped fresh thyme
15 ml / 1 tbsp shredded fresh basil
leaves
120 ml / 4 fl oz / ½ cup dry white wine
450 g / 1 lb raw prawns, peeled and
deveined, or cooked peeled prawns
1.5 kg / 3–3½ lb mussels or clams
(in shells), or a mixture, thoroughly
cleaned
900 g / 2 lb halibut or other firm,
white fish fillets, cut in 5 cm / 2 in
chunks
350 ml / 12 fl oz / 1½ cups fish stock
or water
salt and freshly ground black pepper
extra chopped fresh herbs, to garnish

Serves 6

2

Stir in the tomato purée, canned tomatoes,
herbs and wine. Bring to the boil, lower
the heat and simmer for 20 minutes. Add
the prawns, mussels and/or clams, fish
pieces and stock or water. Season with salt
and pepper to taste.

3

Bring back to the boil, then simmer for
5–6 minutes, until the prawns turn pink, the
fish flakes easily and the mussels and clams
open. If using cooked prawns, add them for
the last 2 minutes only. Serve in large soup
plates, garnished with chopped herbs.

1

Heat the oil in a flameproof casserole. Add
the onions, green pepper, carrots and garlic
and cook for about 5 minutes, until tender.

Cod, Basil and Tomato with a Potato Thatch

With a green salad, this makes an ideal dish for lunch or a family supper.

INGREDIENTS

1 kg / 2 lb smoked cod
1 kg / 2 lb white cod
600 ml / 1 pint milk
2 sprigs basil
1 sprig lemon thyme
75 g / 3 oz butter
1 onion, peeled and chopped
75 g / 3 oz flour
30 ml / 2 tbsp tomato purée
2 tbsp chopped basil
12 medium-sized old potatoes
50 g / 2 oz butter
300 ml / ½ pint milk
salt and pepper
1 tbsp chopped parsley

Serves 8

1

Place both kinds of fish in a roasting pan with the milk, 1.2 litres / 2 pints water and herbs. Simmer for about 3–4 minutes. Leave to cool in the liquid for about 20 minutes. Drain the fish, reserving the liquid for use in the sauce. Flake the fish, taking care to remove any skin and bone, which should be discarded.

2

Melt the butter in a pan, add the onion and cook for about 4 minutes until tender but not browned. Add the flour, tomato purée and half the basil. Gradually add the reserved fish stock, adding a little more milk if necessary to make a fairly thin sauce. Bring this to the boil, season with salt and pepper, and add the remaining basil. Add the fish carefully and stir gently. Pour into an ovenproof dish.

3

Preheat the oven to 180°C/350°F/Gas Mark 4. Boil the potatoes until tender. Add the butter and milk, and mash well. Add salt and pepper to taste and cover the fish, forking to create a pattern. If you like, you can freeze the pie at this stage. Bake for 30 minutes. Serve with chopped parsley.

44

Cod with Lentils and Leeks

This unusual dish is great for entertaining. The vegetables can be cooked ahead of time and the fish baked while the first course is served.

INGREDIENTS

150 g / 5 oz / scant 1 cup green lentils, rinsed
1 bay leaf
1 garlic clove, finely chopped
grated rind of 1 orange
grated rind of 1 lemon
pinch of ground cumin
15 g / ½ oz / 1 tbsp butter
450 g / 1 lb leeks, thinly sliced
300 ml / ½ pint / 1¼ cups whipping cream
15 ml / 1 tbsp lemon juice, or to taste
800 g / 1¾ lb thick cod or haddock fillets, skinned
salt and freshly ground black pepper

Serves 4

1

Put the lentils, bay leaf and garlic in a large saucepan and enough water to cover by 5 cm / 2 in. Bring to the boil, boil gently for 10 minutes, then reduce the heat and simmer for 15–30 minutes more, until the lentils are just tender.

2

Drain the lentils and discard the bay leaf, then stir in half the orange rind and all the lemon rind. Season with the ground cumin and salt and pepper. Transfer to a shallow baking dish or gratin dish. Preheat the oven to 190°C / 375°F / Gas Mark 5.

3

Melt the butter over a medium heat in a saucepan, add the leeks and cook gently, stirring frequently, until just softened. Add 250 ml / 8 fl oz / 1 cup of the cream and the remaining orange rind and cook gently for 15–20 minutes until the leeks have softened completely and the cream has thickened slightly. Stir in the lemon juice and season with salt and plenty of pepper.

4

Cut the fish into four pieces and remove any remaining bones. Season the fish with salt and pepper, place the pieces on top of the lentil mixture and press down slightly. Cover each piece of fish with a quarter of the leek mixture and divide the remaining cream between them. Bake for about 30 minutes until the fish is cooked thoroughly and the topping is golden.

Trout with Almonds

This quick and easy recipe can be cooked for four, adapted by cooking the trout in two frying pans or in batches.

INGREDIENTS

2 trout, about 350 g / 12 oz each, cleaned
40 g / 1½ oz / 6 tbsp plain flour
50 g / 2 oz / ¼ cup butter
25 g / 1 oz / ¼ cup flaked or sliced almonds
30 ml / 2 tbsp dry white wine
salt and freshly ground black pepper

Serves 2

NOTE
The easiest way to coat the trout is to put the flour in a large polythene bag and season with salt and pepper. Place the trout, one at a time, in the bag and shake until evenly coated. Shake off the excess flour from the fish.

1

Coat the trout in the flour, seasoned with salt and pepper. Melt half the butter in a large frying pan. When it is foamy, add the trout and cook for 6–7 minutes on each side, until the skin is golden brown and the flesh next to the bone is opaque. Transfer the fish to warmed plates and keep hot.

2

Add the remaining butter to the pan and cook the almonds until just lightly browned. Add the wine to the pan and boil for 1 minute, stirring constantly, until slightly syrupy. Pour or spoon over the fish and serve at once.

Tuna with Garlic, Tomatoes and Herbs

In France, where this recipe originated, dried wild herbs are used, but fresh herbs are fine.

INGREDIENTS

4 tuna steaks, about 2.5 cm / 1 in thick (175–200 g / 6–7 oz each)
30–45 ml / 2–3 tbsp olive oil
3–4 garlic cloves, finely chopped
60 ml / 4 tbsp dry white wine
3 ripe tomatoes, skinned, seeded and chopped
15–30 ml / 1–2 tbsp dried mixed herbs
salt and freshly ground black pepper
fresh basil leaves, to garnish

Serves 4

NOTE
Tuna is often served pink in the middle. If you prefer it cooked through, reduce the heat and cook for a few extra minutes.

1

Season the tuna steaks with salt and pepper. Set a heavy-based frying pan over a high heat. When very hot, add the oil and swirl to coat. Add the tuna steaks and press down gently, then reduce the heat to medium and cook for 6–8 minutes, turning once, until just slightly pink in the centre.

2

Transfer the steaks to a serving plate and keep hot. Add the garlic to the pan and fry for 15–20 seconds, then pour in the wine and boil until reduced by half. Add the tomatoes and herbs and cook for 2–3 minutes. Season with pepper and pour over the fish steaks. Serve, garnished with fresh basil leaves.

Pan-fried Garlic Sardines

Lightly fry a sliced clove of garlic to garnish the fish. This dish could also be made with sprats or fresh anchovies if available.

INGREDIENTS

8 fresh sardines
30 ml / 2 tbsp olive oil
4 garlic cloves
finely grated rind of 2 lemons
30 ml / 2 tbsp chopped fresh parsley
salt and freshly ground black pepper

For the tomato bread
2 large ripe beefsteak tomatoes
8 slices crusty bread, toasted

Serves 4

1

Gut and clean the sardines. Pat them dry with kitchen paper.

2

Heat the oil in a frying pan and cook the garlic cloves until soft.

3

Remove the garlic from the pan, then fry the sardines for 4–5 minutes. Sprinkle over the lemon rind, parsley and seasoning.

4

Cut the tomatoes in half and rub them on to the toast. Discard the skins. Serve each sardine on a slice of the tomato toast.

Grilled Sea Bass with Fennel

Fennel has an unmistakable flavour, and goes particularly well with fish.

INGREDIENTS

*1 sea bass, 1.75 kg / 4–4½ lb,
cleaned
60–90 ml / 4–6 tbsp olive oil
10–15 ml / 2–3 tsp fennel seeds
2 large fennel bulbs, with fronds
attached
60 ml / 4 tbsp Pernod
salt and freshly ground black pepper*

Serves 6–8

1

With a sharp knife, make three or four deep cuts in both sides of the fish. Brush the fish with olive oil and season with salt and pepper. Sprinkle the fennel seeds in the stomach cavity and in the cuts. Set aside while you cook the fennel.

2

Preheat the grill. Trim the fennel fronds and quarter the bulbs lengthways. Remove the core and slice thinly. Reserve the fennel fronds. Put the fennel slices on the grill rack and brush with oil. Grill for 4 minutes on each side until tender. Transfer to a large dish or platter.

3

Place the fish on the oiled grill rack and position about 13 cm / 5 in from the heat. Grill for 10–12 minutes on each side, brushing occasionally with oil. Transfer the fish to the platter on top of the fennel. Garnish with the fennel fronds. Heat the Pernod in a small pan, light it and pour it, flaming, over the fish. Serve at once.

Crab Cakes

These crab cakes are full of flavour thanks to mustard, horseradish and Worcestershire sauce.

INGREDIENTS

450 g / 1 lb fresh white crab meat
1 egg, well beaten
5 ml / 1 tsp Dijon mustard
10 ml / 2 tsp prepared horseradish
10 ml / 2 tsp Worcestershire sauce
8 spring onions, finely chopped
45 ml / 3 tbsp chopped fresh parsley
75 g / 3 oz / 1½ cups fresh breadcrumbs
15 ml / 1 tbsp whipping cream
(optional)
115 g / 4 oz / 1 cup dry breadcrumbs
40 g / 1½ oz / 3 tbsp butter
salt and freshly ground black pepper
lemon wedges and fresh dill sprigs, for
serving

Serves 3–6

1

In a mixing bowl, combine the crab meat, egg, mustard, horseradish, Worcestershire sauce, spring onions, parsley and fresh breadcrumbs. Mix gently, leaving the pieces of crab meat as large as possible. Season to taste. If the mixture is too dry to hold together, add the cream. Divide the crab mixture into six portions and shape into round, flat cakes.

2

Spread out the dry breadcrumbs on a plate. Coat the crab cakes on both sides. Melt the butter in a frying pan. Fry the crab cakes for about 3 minutes on each side or until golden. Add more fat if necessary. Serve with lemon wedges and dill.

Baked Stuffed Crab

Good cooking means meals that are good looking as well as tasty. This recipe scores on all counts.

INGREDIENTS

4 freshly cooked crabs
1 celery stick, diced
1 spring onion, finely chopped
1 small fresh green chilli, seeded and
finely chopped
75 ml / 5 tbsp mayonnaise
30 ml / 2 tbsp fresh lemon juice
15 ml / 1 tbsp snipped fresh chives
25 g / 1 oz / ½ cup fresh breadcrumbs
50 g / 2 oz / ½ cup grated Cheddar
cheese
25 g / 1 oz / 2 tbsp butter, melted
salt and freshly ground black pepper
fresh parsley sprigs, to garnish

Serves 4

1

Preheat the oven to 190°C / 375°F / Gas Mark 3. Remove the meat from the crab body and claws. Reserve the whole shells.

2

Scrub the crab shells. Cut open the seam on the underside with scissors. The inner part of the shell should break off cleanly along the seam. Rinse the shells and dry them well.

3

In a bowl, combine the crab meat, celery, spring onion, chilli, mayonnaise, lemon juice and chives. Season and mix. In a separate bowl, toss together the breadcrumbs, cheese and melted butter.

4

Pile the crab mixture into the shells. Sprinkle with the cheese mixture. Bake for about 20 minutes until golden brown. Serve hot, garnished with parsley.

MEAT & POULTRY

Pork Sausage and Puff Pastry Plait

Country butchers sell a wonderful variety of sausages, including venison, pork and apple, and herb. All taste delicious when wrapped around a wild mushroom filling and baked in pastry.

INGREDIENTS

50 g / 2 oz / 4 tbsp butter
½ garlic clove, crushed
15 ml / 1 tbsp chopped fresh thyme
450 g / 1 lb assorted wild and
cultivated mushrooms, sliced
50 g / 2 oz / 1 cup fresh white
breadcrumbs
75 ml / 5 tbsp chopped fresh parsley
350 g / 12 oz puff pastry
675 g / 1½ lb best pork sausages
1 egg, beaten with a pinch of salt
salt and freshly ground black pepper

Serves 4

3

Make a series of slanting 2.5 cm / 1 in cuts in the pastry on either side of the filling. Fold each end of the pastry over the filling, moisten the pastry with beaten egg and then cross the top with alternate strips of pastry from each side. Allow the plait to rest for 40 minutes. Preheat the oven to 180°C / 350°F / Gas Mark 4. Brush the plait with a little more egg and bake for 1 hour.

1

Melt the butter in a large frying pan and soften the garlic, thyme and mushrooms gently for 5–6 minutes. When the mushroom juices begin to run, increase the heat to drive off the liquid, then stir in the breadcrumbs, parsley and seasoning.

2

Roll out the pastry on a floured surface to a 36 x 25 cm / 14 x 10 in rectangle. Place on a large baking sheet. Skin the sausages. Place half of the sausagemeat in a 13 cm / 5 in strip along the centre of the pastry. Cover with the mushroom mixture, then with the rest of the sausagemeat.

Lamb Stew with Vegetables

This farmhouse stew is made with lamb and a selection of young tender spring vegetables such as carrots, new potatoes, baby onions, peas, French beans and especially turnips!

INGREDIENTS

60 ml / 4 tbsp vegetable oil
1.5 kg / 3–3½ lb lamb shoulder, trimmed and cut into 5 cm / 2 in pieces
120 ml / 4 fl oz / ½ cup water
45–60 ml / 3–4 tbsp plain flour
1 litre / 1¾ pints / 4 cups lamb stock
1 large bouquet garni
3 garlic cloves, lightly crushed
3 ripe tomatoes, skinned, seeded and chopped
5 ml / 1 tsp tomato purée
675 g / 1½ lb small potatoes, peeled or scrubbed
12 baby carrots, scrubbed

115 g / 4 oz French beans, cut into 5 cm / 2 in pieces
25 g / 1 oz / 2 tbsp butter
12–18 baby onions or shallots, peeled
6 medium turnips, quartered
30 ml / 2 tbsp granulated sugar
¼ tsp dried thyme
175 g / 6 oz / 1¼ cups peas
50 g / 2 oz / ½ cup mangetouts
salt and freshly ground pepper
45 ml / 3 tbsp chopped fresh parsley or coriander, to garnish

Serves 6

1

Heat half the oil in a large, heavy-based frying pan. Brown the lamb in batches, adding more oil if needed, and place it in a large, flameproof casserole. Add 45 ml / 3 tbsp of the water to the pan and boil for about 1 minute, stirring and scraping the base of the pan, then pour the liquid into the casserole.

2

Sprinkle the flour over the browned meat in the casserole and set it over a medium heat. Cook for 3–5 minutes until browned. Stir in the stock, the bouquet garni, garlic, tomatoes and tomato purée. Season with salt and pepper.

3

Bring to the boil over a high heat. Skim the surface, reduce the heat and simmer, stirring occasionally, for about 1 hour until the meat is tender. Cool the stew to room temperature, cover and chill overnight.

4

About 1½ hours before serving, take the casserole from the fridge, lift off the solid fat and blot the surface with kitchen paper to remove all traces of fat. Set the casserole over a medium heat and bring to a simmer. Cook the potatoes in a pan of boiling, salted water for 15–20 minutes, then transfer to a bowl and add the carrots to the same water. Cook for 4–5 minutes and transfer to the same bowl. Add the French beans and boil for 2–3 minutes. Transfer to the bowl with the other vegetables.

5

(Left) Melt the butter in a heavy-based frying pan and add the onions and turnips with a further 45 ml / 3 tbsp water. Cover and cook for 4–5 minutes. Stir in the sugar and thyme and cook until the vegetables are caramelized. Transfer them to the bowl of vegetables. Add the remaining water to the pan. Boil for 1 minute, incorporating the sediment, then add to the lamb.

6

When the lamb and gravy are hot, add the cooked vegetables to the stew and stir gently to distribute. Stir in the peas and mangetouts and cook for 5 minutes until they turn a bright green, then stir in 30 ml / 2 tbsp of the parsley or coriander. Pour the stew into a large, warmed serving dish. Scatter over the remaining parsley or coriander and serve.

Roast Leg of Lamb with Wild Mushroom Stuffing

*Removing the thigh bone creates a cavity that can be filled with
a wild mushroom stuffing – the perfect treat for Sunday lunch.*

INGREDIENTS

1.75 kg / 4–4½ lb leg of lamb, boned
salt and freshly ground black pepper
watercress, to garnish

For the wild mushroom stuffing
25 g / 1 oz / 2 tbsp butter
1 shallot or small onion, chopped
225 g / 8 oz / 2 cups assorted wild
and cultivated mushrooms

½ garlic clove, crushed
1 fresh thyme sprig, chopped
25 g / 1 oz crustless white
bread, diced
2 egg yolks

For the wild mushroom gravy
60 ml / 4 tbsp red wine
400 ml / 14 fl oz / 1⅔ cups hot

chicken stock
5 g / 2 tbsp dried ceps, soaked in
boiling water for 20 minutes
20 ml / 4 tsp cornflour
5 ml / 1 tsp Dijon mustard
15 ml / 1 tbsp water
½ tsp wine vinegar
knob of butter

Serves 4

1

Preheat the oven to 200°C / 400°F / Gas
Mark 6. To make the stuffing, melt the
butter in a large, non-stick frying pan and
gently fry the shallot or onion without
colouring. Add the mushrooms, garlic and
thyme. Stir until the mushroom juices
begin to run, then increase the heat so that
they evaporate completely.

4

Place the lamb in a roasting tin. Roast for
15 minutes per 450 g /1 lb for rare meat
and 20 minutes per 450 g / 1 lb for
medium-rare. A 1.8 kg / 4 lb leg will take
1 hour 20 minutes if cooked medium-rare.

2

Transfer the mushrooms to a mixing bowl
and add the bread and egg yolks. Season
with salt and pepper and mix well. Allow
to cool slightly.

5

Transfer the lamb to a warmed serving
plate. Spoon off all excess fat from the
roasting tin and brown the sediment over a
medium heat. Add the wine and stir in the
chicken stock and the mushrooms, with
their soaking liquid.

3

Season the inside of the lamb cavity, then
spoon in the stuffing. Tie up the end with
fine string and then tie around the joint so
that it does not lose its shape.

6

Mix the cornflour and mustard in a cup;
blend in the water. Stir into the stock and
thicken. Add the vinegar. Season and stir in
the butter. Garnish the lamb with
watercress and serve with the wild
mushroom gravy.

Lamb Pie with Pear, Ginger and Mint Sauce

Cooking lamb with fruit is an idea taken from traditional Persian cuisine.

INGREDIENTS

1 boned mid-loin of lamb, 1 kg/2 lb
after boning
salt and pepper
8 large sheets filo pastry
25 g/1 oz/scant 2 tbsp butter

For the stuffing
1 tbsp butter
1 small onion, chopped
115 g/4 oz wholemeal breadcrumbs
grated rind of 1 lemon
170 g/6 oz drained canned pears from

a 400 g/14 oz can (rest
of can, and juice, used for sauce)
¼ tsp ground ginger
1 small egg, beaten
skewers, string and large needle to
make roll

For the sauce
rest of can of pears, including juice
2 tsp finely chopped fresh mint

Serves 6

1

Prepare the stuffing. Melt the butter in a pan and add the onion, cooking until soft. Preheat the oven to 180°C/350°F/Gas Mark 4. Put the butter and onion into a mixing bowl and add the breadcrumbs, lemon rind, pears and ginger. Season lightly and add enough beaten egg to bind.

2

Spread the loin out flat, fat side down, and season. Place the stuffing along the middle of the loin and roll carefully, holding with skewers while you sew it together with string. Heat a large baking pan in the oven and brown the loin slowly on all sides. This will take 20–30 minutes. Leave to cool, and store in the refrigerator until needed.

3

Preheat the oven to 200°C/400°F/Gas Mark 6. Take two sheets of filo pastry and brush with melted butter. Overlap by about 13 cm/5 in to make a square. Place the next two sheets on top and brush with butter. Continue until all the pastry has been used.

4

Place the roll of lamb diagonally across one corner of the pastry, without overlapping the sides. Fold the corner over the lamb, fold in the sides, and brush the pastry well with melted butter. Roll to the far corner of the sheet. Place join side down on a buttered baking sheet and brush all over with the rest of the melted butter. Bake for about 30 minutes or until golden brown.

5

Blend the remaining pears with their juice and the mint, and serve with the lamb.

Country Meat Loaf

This dish makes a delicious alternative to a joint of meat.

INGREDIENTS

25 g / 1 oz / 2 tbsp butter
1 small onion, finely chopped
2 garlic cloves, crushed
2 celery sticks, finely chopped
450 g / 1 lb / 2 cups minced lean beef
450 g / 1 lb / 2 cups minced pork
2 eggs
*50 g / 2 oz / 1 cup fresh white
breadcrumbs*
45 ml / 3 tbsp chopped fresh parsley
30 ml / 2 tbsp snipped fresh basil
½ tsp fresh thyme leaves
½ tsp salt
½ tsp freshly ground black pepper
30 ml / 2 tbsp Worcestershire sauce
60 ml / 4 tbsp chilli sauce or ketchup
6 rindless streaky bacon rashers
fresh basil sprigs, to garnish

Serve 6

3

Use your hands to shape the meat mixture into an oval loaf. Carefully transfer it to a roasting tin.

4

Lay the bacon slices across the meat loaf. Bake for 1¼ hours, basting occasionally. Remove from the oven and drain off the fat. Place the meat loaf on a platter and leave to stand for 10 minutes before serving, garnished with basil.

1

Preheat the oven to 180°C / 350°F / Gas Mark 4. Melt the butter in a small frying pan. Cook the onion, garlic and celery over a low heat for 8–10 minutes until softened. Remove from the heat and leave to cool slightly.

2

In a large mixing bowl combine the onion, garlic and celery with all the other ingredients except the bacon. Mix together lightly.

Sunday Best Beef Wellington

For a special occasion, nothing surpasses the succulent flavour of Beef Wellington.
Traditionally, the beef is spread with goose liver pâté, but many country cooks prefer a pâté
made from woodland mushrooms, especially when they have picked them themselves.

INGREDIENTS

675 g / 1½ lb fillet steak, tied
15 ml / 1 tbsp vegetable oil
350 g / 12 oz puff pastry
1 egg, beaten, to glaze
salt and freshly ground black pepper

For the parsley pancakes
50 g / 2 oz / ½ cup plain flour
150 ml / ¼ pint / ⅔ cup milk
1 egg
30 ml / 2 tbsp chopped fresh parsley

For the mushroom pâté
25 g / 1 oz / 2 tbsp butter
2 shallots or 1 small onion, chopped
450 g / 1 lb / 4 cups assorted wild
and cultivated mushrooms, chopped
50 g / 2 oz / 1 cup fresh white
breadcrumbs
75 ml / 5 tbsp double cream
2 egg yolks

Serves 4

1

Preheat the oven to 220°C / 425°F / Gas Mark 7. Season the fillet steak with several twists of black pepper. Heat the oil in a roasting tin, add the steak and quickly sear to brown all sides. Transfer to the oven and roast for 15 minutes for rare, 20 minutes for medium-rare or 25 minutes for well-done meat. Set aside to cool. Reduce the oven temperature to 190°C / 375°F / Gas Mark 5.

2

To make the pancakes, beat the flour, a pinch of salt, half the milk, the egg and parsley together until smooth, then stir in the remaining milk. Heat a greased, non-stick pan and pour in enough batter to coat the bottom. When set, turn the pancake over and cook the other side briefly until lightly browned. Continue with the remaining batter – the recipe makes three or four pancakes.

3

To make the mushroom pâté, melt the butter in a frying pan and fry the shallots or onion for 7–10 minutes to soften without colouring. Add the mushrooms and cook until the juices run. Increase the heat so that the juices evaporate. Combine the breadcrumbs, cream and egg yolks. Add to the mushroom mixture and mix to a smooth paste. Allow to cool.

4

Roll out the pastry to a 36 x 30 cm / 14 x 12 in rectangle. Place two pancakes on the pastry and spread with mushroom pâté. Place the beef on top and spread over any remaining pâté, then the remaining pancakes. Cut out and reserve four squares from the corners of the pastry, then moisten the pastry with egg and wrap the meat. Decorate with the reserved pastry trimmings.

5

Put the Beef Wellington on a baking sheet and brush evenly with beaten egg. Bake for about 40 minutes until golden brown. To ensure that the meat is heated through, test with a meat thermometer. It should read 52–54°C / 125–130°F for rare, 57°C / 135°F for medium-rare and 71°C / 160°F for well-done meat.

Traditional Beef Stew and Dumplings

This dish can cook in the oven while you go for a wintry walk to work up an appetite.

INGREDIENTS

25 g / 1 oz / 1 tbsp plain flour
1.2 kg / 2½ lb stewing steak, cubed
30 ml / 2 tbsp olive oil
2 large onions, sliced
450 g / 1 lb carrots, sliced
300 ml / ½ pint / 1¼ cup Guinness
or dark beer
3 bay leaves
10 ml / 2 tsp brown sugar
3 fresh thyme sprigs
5 ml / 1 tsp cider vinegar
salt and freshly ground black pepper

For the dumplings
115 g / 4 oz / ½ cup grated hard
white fat
225 g / 8 oz / 2 cups self-raising
flour
30 ml / 2 tbsp chopped mixed
fresh herbs
about 150 ml / ¼ pint / ⅔ cup water

Serves 6

1

Preheat the oven to 160°C / 325°F /
Gas Mark 3. Season the flour and sprinkle
over the meat, tossing to coat.

2

Heat the oil in a large casserole and lightly
sauté the onions and carrots. Remove the
vegetables using a slotted spoon and
reserve them.

3

Brown the meat well in batches
in the casserole.

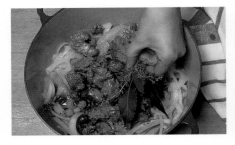

4

Return all the vegetables to the casserole
and add any leftover seasoned flour. Add
the Guinness or beer, bay leaves, sugar and
thyme. Bring the liquid to the boil and then
transfer to the oven. Leave the meat to cook
for 1 hour and 40 minutes, before making
the dumplings.

5

Mix the grated fat, flour and herbs
together. Add enough water to make
a soft sticky dough.

6

Form the dough into small balls with floured
hands. Add the cider vinegar to the meat
and spoon the dumplings on top. Cook for
a further 20 minutes, until the dumplings
are cooked through, and serve hot.

Steak and Kidney Pie, with Mustard and Bay Gravy

This is a sharpened-up, bay-flavoured version of a traditional favourite. The fragrant mustard, bay and parsley perfectly complement the flavour of the beef.

INGREDIENTS

450 g / 1 lb puff pastry
2½ tbsp flour
salt and pepper
750 g / 1½ lb rump steak, cubed
170 g / 6 oz pig's or lamb's kidney
25 g / 1 oz / scant 2 tbsp butter
1 medium onion, chopped
1 tbsp made English mustard
2 bay leaves
1 tbsp chopped parsley
150 ml / 5 fl oz beef stock
1 egg, beaten

Serves 4

1

Roll out two-thirds of the pastry on a floured surface to about 3 mm / ⅛ in thick. Line a 1.5 litre / 2½ pint pie dish. Place a pie funnel in the middle.

2

Put the flour, salt and pepper in a bowl and toss the cubes of steak in the mixture. Remove all fat and skin from the kidneys, and slice thickly. Add to the steak cubes and toss well. Melt the butter in a pan and fry the chopped onion until soft, then add the mustard, bay leaves, parsley and stock and stir well.

3

Preheat the oven to 190°C / 375°F / Gas Mark 5. Place the steak and kidney in the pie and add the stock mixture. Roll out the remaining pastry to a thickness of 3 mm / ⅛ in. Brush the edges of the pastry forming the lower half of the pie with beaten egg and cover with the second piece of pastry. Press the pieces of pastry together to seal the edges, then trim. Use the trimmings to decorate the top with a pattern of leaves.

4

Brush the whole pie with beaten egg and make a small hole over the top of the funnel. Bake for about 1 hour until the pastry is golden brown.

Beef Casserole with Beans

This hearty casserole is slow cooked to ensure that the meat is beautifully tender.

INGREDIENTS

*225 g / 8 oz / 1¼ cups haricot or
butter beans, soaked overnight in water
30–60 ml / 2–4 tbsp oil
10 small onions, halved
2 carrots, diced
1.5 kg / 3–3½ lb stewing steak, cubed
6 small hard-boiled eggs in their shells
5 ml / 1 tsp paprika
5 ml / 1 tsp tomato purée
600 ml / 1 pint / 2½ cups boiling
water or beef stock
salt and freshly ground black pepper*

Serves 6–8

NOTE

If you have one, use a large slow cooker for
cooking the stew. You should not need to
add extra liquid.

___1___

Preheat the oven to 110°C / 225°F / Gas
Mark ¼. Drain the beans, place them in a
saucepan and cover with fresh water. Bring
to the boil. Cook rapidly for 10 minutes,
skimming off the white froth and any bean
skins that come to the surface. Drain.

___2___

Heat half the oil in a frying pan and sauté the
onions for about 10 minutes, then transfer to
a casserole, with the carrots and beans. Heat
the remaining oil and brown the beef in
batches. Place it on top of the vegetables.
Tuck the eggs between the pieces of meat.

___3___

Stir the paprika and tomato purée into the
oil left in the pan. Add a generous
sprinkling of salt and pepper and cook for
1 minute. Stir in the boiling water or stock
to incorporate the sediment, then pour the
mixture over the meat and eggs.

___4___

Cover the casserole and cook the cholent for
at least 8 hours or until the meat is very
tender, adding more liquid as needed. Take
out the eggs, remove the shells and return
them to the casserole before serving.

Traditional Chicken Pie

With its golden crust and rich chicken and vegetable filling, an old-fashioned chicken pie is a favourite family dish.

INGREDIENTS

50 g / 2 oz / 4 tbsp butter
1 onion, chopped
3 carrots, diced
1 parsnip, diced
20 g / ¾ oz / 3 tbsp plain flour
350 ml / 12 fl oz / 1½ cups chicken stock
75 ml / 5 tbsp medium sherry
75 ml / 5 tbsp dry white wine
175 ml / 6 fl oz / ¾ cup whipping cream
115 g / 4 oz / ¾ cup frozen peas, thawed
350 g / 12 oz cooked chicken meat, in chunks
5 ml / 1 tsp dried thyme

15 ml / 1 tbsp finely chopped fresh parsley
salt and freshly ground black pepper
1 egg, beaten with 30 ml / 2 tbsp milk, to glaze

For the pastry
175 g / 6 oz / 1½ cups plain flour
½ tsp salt
115 g / 4 oz / ½ cup lard or vegetable fat
30–45 ml / 2–3 tbsp iced water

Serves 6

1

For the pastry, sift the flour and salt into a mixing bowl. Rub in the fat until the mixture resembles coarse breadcrumbs, then add enough iced water to form a dough. Dust with flour, wrap and chill.

2

Preheat the oven to 200°C / 400°F / Gas Mark 6. Heat half the butter in a saucepan. Add the onion, carrots and parsnip and cook for 10 minutes, until softened. Remove from the pan with a slotted spoon.

3

Melt the remaining butter in the pan. Add the flour and cook for 2 minutes, stirring constantly. Stir in the stock, sherry and white wine. Bring the sauce to the boil, and cook for 1 minute, stirring constantly.

4

Stir the cream, peas, chicken, thyme and parsley into the sauce. Season to taste with salt and pepper. Simmer for 1 minute, stirring, then transfer the mixture to a 2 litre / 3½ pint / 8 cup pie dish.

5

Roll out the pastry. Cover the pie and trim off the excess pastry. Dampen the rim of the dish. With a fork, press the pastry to the rim to seal. Cut decorative shapes from the pastry trimmings. Brush the pastry all over with the egg glaze. Arrange the pastry shapes on top.

6

Brush again with the egg glaze. Make one or two holes in the crust so steam can escape during baking. Bake the pie for about 35 minutes, until the pastry is golden brown. Serve hot.

Chicken and Sweetcorn Stew

Americans would serve this rustic stew with biscuits, which resemble what the British call scones. The combination works remarkably well.

INGREDIENTS

1.75 kg / 4 lb chicken, cut in serving
pieces
paprika
30 ml / 2 tbsp olive oil
25 g / 1 oz / 2 tbsp butter
450 g / 1 lb onions, chopped
1 green or yellow pepper, cored, seeded
and chopped
400 g / 14 oz can chopped tomatoes
250 ml / 8 fl oz / 1 cup white wine
475 ml / 16 fl oz / 2 cups chicken
stock or water
45 ml / 3 tbsp chopped fresh parsley
½ tsp Tabasco sauce
15 ml / 1 tbsp Worcestershire sauce
275 g / 10 oz / 2 cups sweetcorn
kernels (fresh, frozen, or drained
canned)
150 g / 5 oz / 1 cup broad beans
(fresh or frozen)
20 g / ¾ oz / 3 tbsp plain flour
salt and freshly ground black pepper
flat leaf parsley sprigs, to garnish

Serves 6

___1___

Rinse the chicken pieces under cool water and pat dry with kitchen paper. Sprinkle each piece lightly with salt and paprika.

___2___

Heat the oil and butter in a large, heavy-based saucepan. Add the chicken pieces and fry until golden brown on all sides. Remove with tongs and set aside.

___3___

Reduce the heat to low and cook the onions and pepper for 8–10 minutes, until softened. Stir in the tomatoes, wine, stock or water, parsley and sauces. Turn up the heat and bring to the boil.

___4___

Return the chicken to the pan, pushing it down in the sauce. Cover, reduce the heat and simmer for 30 minutes, stirring occasionally.

___5___

Add the corn and beans and mix well. Partly cover and cook for 30 minutes more. Skim off or blot any surface fat.

___6___

Mix the flour with a little water to make a paste. Gradually add 175 ml / 6 fl oz / ¾ cup of the hot liquid from the pan. Stir this mixture into the stew and season with salt and pepper. Cook for 5–8 minutes more, stirring occasionally. Garnish and serve.

Chicken with Sloe Gin and Juniper

Juniper is used in the manufacture of gin, and this dish is flavoured with both sloe gin and juniper. Sloe gin is easy to make and has a wonderful flavour, but it can also be bought ready-made.

INGREDIENTS

2 tbsp butter
30 ml / 2 tbsp sunflower oil
8 chicken breast fillets, skinned
350 g / 12 oz carrots, cooked
1 clove garlic, peeled and crushed
1 tbsp finely chopped parsley
60 ml / 2 fl oz / ¼ cup chicken stock
60 ml / 2 fl oz / ¼ cup red wine
60 ml / 2 fl oz / ¼ cup sloe gin
1 tsp crushed juniper berries
salt and pepper
1 bunch basil, to garnish

Serves 8

___
1

Melt the butter with the oil in a pan, and sauté the chicken fillets until they are browned on all sides.

___
2

In a food processor, combine all the remaining ingredients except the basil, and blend to a smooth purée. If the mixture seems too thick add a little more red wine or water until a thinner consistency is reached.

___
3

Put the chicken breasts in a pan, pour the sauce over the top and cook until the chicken is cooked through, which should take about 15 minutes. Adjust the seasoning and serve garnished with chopped fresh basil leaves.

Duck Stew with Olives

In this traditional method of preparing duck the sweetness of the shallots balances the saltiness of the olives.

INGREDIENTS

2 ducks, about 1.4 kg / 3¼ lb each, quartered, or 8 duck leg quarters
225 g / 8 oz / 1½ cups shallots, peeled
30 ml / 2 tbsp plain flour
350 ml / 12 fl oz / 1½ cups dry red wine
475 ml / 16 fl oz / 2 cups duck or chicken stock
1 bouquet garni
115 g / 4 oz / 1 cup stoned green or black olives, or a combination
salt, if needed, and freshly ground black pepper

Serves 6–8

1

Put the duck portions, skin side down, in a large frying pan. Cook over a medium heat for 10–12 minutes until well browned, then turn to colour evenly. Cook in batches if necessary.

2

Pour 15 ml / 1 tbsp of the duck fat into a large, flameproof casserole. Place the casserole over a medium heat and cook the shallots until evenly browned, stirring frequently. Sprinkle with the flour and cook for 2 minutes more, stirring frequently.

3

Stir in the wine, then add the duck pieces, stock and bouquet garni. Bring to the boil, then reduce the heat, cover and simmer for about 40 minutes, stirring occasionally.

4

Rinse the olives in several changes of cold water. If they are very salty, put them in a saucepan, cover with water and bring to the boil, then drain and rinse. Add the stoned olives to the casserole and continue cooking for 20 minutes more, until the duck is very tender.

5

Transfer the duck pieces, shallots and olives to a plate. Strain the cooking liquid, skim off all the fat and return the liquid to the pan. Boil to reduce by about one-third, then adjust the seasoning and return the duck and vegetables to the casserole. Simmer gently for a few minutes to heat through and serve.

Roast Turkey with Mushroom Stuffing

A fresh farm turkey tastes wonderful with a wild mushroom stuffing.
Serve it with a wild mushroom gravy for maximum impact.

INGREDIENTS

5 kg / 11 lb free range turkey, dressed
weight
butter, for basting
watercress, to garnish

For the mushroom stuffing
50 g / 2 oz / 4 tbsp butter
1 onion, chopped
225 g / 8 oz wild mushrooms, chopped
75 g / 3 oz / 1½ cups fresh white
breadcrumbs
115 g / 4 oz pork sausages, skinned
1 small fresh truffle, sliced (optional)
5 drops truffle oil (optional)
salt and freshly ground black pepper

For the gravy
75 ml / 5 tbsp medium sherry
400 ml / 14 fl oz / 1⅔ cups chicken stock
20 ml / 4 tsp cornflour
5 ml / 1 tsp Dijon mustard
10 ml / 2 tsp water
½ tsp red wine vinegar

Serves 6–8

1

Preheat the oven to 220°C / 425°F / Gas
Mark 7. To make the stuffing, melt the
butter in a saucepan and fry the onion
gently without colouring. Add the
mushrooms and stir until their juices begin
to flow. Transfer from the pan to a bowl
and add all the remaining ingredients,
including the truffle and truffle oil if using.
Season and stir well to combine.

2

Spoon the stuffing into the neck cavity of
the turkey and enclose, fastening the skin
on the underside with a skewer.

3

Rub the skin of the turkey with butter,
place in a large roasting tin and roast for
50 minutes. Lower the temperature to
180°C / 350°F / Gas Mark 4 and cook for
2½ hours more.

4

Transfer the turkey to a carving board,
cover loosely with foil and keep hot. Spoon
off the fat from the roasting juices, then
place the tin over a medium heat until the
juices are reduced to a sediment. Stir in the
sherry and incorporate the sediment, then
stir in the chicken stock.

5

Place the cornflour and mustard in a small
bowl. Stir in the water and wine vinegar.
Stir this mixture into the juices in the
roasting tin and simmer to thicken. Season
and stir in a knob of butter. Garnish the
turkey with watercress. Pour the gravy into
a serving jug and serve separately.

DESSERTS

Apple Mint and Pink Grapefruit Fool

Apple mint can easily run riot in the herb garden; this is an excellent
way of using up an abundant crop.

INGREDIENTS

500 g / 1 lb tart apples, peeled, cored
and sliced
225 g / 8 oz pink grapefruit segments
45 ml / 3 tbsp clear honey
30 ml / 2 tbsp water
6 large sprigs apple mint, plus more
to garnish
150 ml / ¼ pint / ⅔ cup double cream
300 ml / ½ pint / 1¼ cups custard

Serves 4–6

1

Place the apples, grapefruit, honey, water
and apple mint in a pan, cover and simmer
for 10 minutes until soft. Leave in the pan
to cool, then discard the apple mint. Purée
the mixture in a food processor.

2

Whip the cream until it forms soft peaks,
and fold into the custard, keeping 2 tbsp to
decorate. Carefully fold the cream into the
fruit mixture. Serve chilled and decorated
with swirls of cream and sprigs of mint.

Summer Fruit Gâteau with Heartsease

No one could resist the appeal of little heartsease pansies. This cake would be lovely for a sentimental summer occasion in the garden.

INGREDIENTS

100 g / 3½ oz / scant ½ cup soft margarine, plus more to grease mould
100 g / 3¾ oz / scant ½ cup sugar
10 ml / 2 tsp clear honey
150 g / 5 oz / 1¼ cups self-raising flour
3 ml / ½ tsp baking powder
30 ml / 2 tbsp milk
2 eggs, plus white of one more for crystallizing
15 ml / 1 tbsp rosewater
15 ml / 1 tbsp Cointreau
16 heartsease flowers
caster sugar, as required, to crystallize
icing sugar, to decorate
500 g / 1 lb strawberries
strawberry leaves, to decorate

Serves 6–8

1

Crystallize the flowers by painting them with lightly beaten egg white and sprinkling with caster sugar. Leave to dry.

2

Preheat the oven to 190°C / 375°F / Gas Mark 5. Grease and lightly flour a ring mould.

3

Take a large mixing bowl and add the soft margarine, sugar, honey, flour, baking powder, milk and 2 eggs to the mixing bowl and beat well for 1 minute. Add the rosewater and the Cointreau and mix well.

4

Pour the mixture into the tin and bake for 40 minutes. Allow to stand for a few minutes and then turn out on to the plate that you wish to serve it on.

5

Sift icing sugar over the cake. Fill the centre of the ring with strawberries. Decorate with crystallized heartsease flowers and some strawberry leaves.

Borage, Mint and Lemon Balm Sorbet

Borage has such a pretty flower head that it is worth growing just to make this recipe, and to float the flowers in summer drinks. The sorbet itself has a very refreshing, delicate taste, perfect for a hot afternoon.

INGREDIENTS

500 g / 1 lb / 2⅛ cups sugar
500 ml / 17 fl oz / 2⅛ cups water
6 sprigs mint, plus more to decorate
6 lemon balm leaves
250 ml / 8 fl oz / 1 cup white wine
30 ml / 2 tbsp lemon juice
borage sprigs, to decorate

Serves 6–8

1

Place the sugar and water in a saucepan with the washed herbs. Bring to the boil. Remove from the heat and add the wine. Cover and cool. Chill for several hours, then add the lemon juice. Freeze: as soon as the mixture begins to freeze, stir it briskly and replace in the freezer. Repeat every 15 minutes for at least 3 hours.

3

Place a smaller freezer-proof bowl inside each larger bowl and put a heavy weight inside such as a metal weight from some scales. Fill with more cooled boiled water, float more herbs in this and freeze.

2

To make the small ice bowls, pour about 1 cm/½ in cold, boiled water into small freezer-proof bowls, about 600 ml/ 1 pint/1¼ US pints in capacity, and arrange some herbs in the water. Freeze, then add a little more water to cover the herbs.

4

To release the ice bowls, warm the inner bowl with a small amount of very hot water and twist it out. Warm the outer bowl by standing it in very hot water for a few seconds, then tip out the ice bowl. Spoon the sorbet into the ice bowls, decorate with sprigs of mint and borage and serve.

French Apple Tart

For added flavour, scatter some toasted, flaked almonds over the top of this classic tart.

INGREDIENTS

For the pastry
115 g / 4 oz / ½ cup unsalted
butter, softened
50 g / 2 oz / 4 tbsp vanilla sugar
1 egg
225 g / 8 oz / 2 cups plain flour

For the filling
50 g / 2 oz / 4 tbsp unsalted butter
5 large tart apples, peeled, cored
and sliced
juice of ½ lemon
300 ml / ½ pint / 1¼ cups double cream
2 egg yolks
25 g / 1 oz / 2 tbsp vanilla sugar
50 g / 2 oz / ⅔ cup ground
almonds, toasted
25 g / 1 oz / 2 tbsp flaked almonds,
toasted, to garnish

Serves 8

1

Place the butter and sugar in a food
processor and process well together.
Add the egg and process to mix it in well.

2

Add the flour and process until you have
a soft dough. Wrap the dough in clear film
and chill it for 30 minutes.

3

Roll the pastry out on a lightly floured
surface to about 22–25 cm / 9–10 in diameter.

4

Line a flan tin with the pastry and chill it
for a further 30 minutes. Preheat the oven
to 220°C / 425°F / Gas Mark 7 and place a
baking sheet in the oven to heat up. Line the
pastry case with greaseproof paper and
baking beans and bake blind on the baking
sheet for 10 minutes. Remove the beans
and paper, and cook for a further 5 minutes.

5

Turn the oven down to 190°C / 375°F /
Gas Mark 5. To make the filling, melt the
butter in a frying pan and lightly sauté
the apples for 5–7 minutes. Sprinkle the
apples with lemon juice.

6

Beat the cream and egg yolks with the
sugar. Stir in the toasted ground almonds.
Arrange the apple slices on top of the warm
pastry and pour over the cream mixture.
Bake for 25 minutes, or until the cream is
just set – it tastes better if the cream is still
slightly runny in the centre. Serve hot or
cold, scattered with flaked almonds.

Spiced Red Fruit Compote

When summer fruits are at their best, what could be nicer than a simple compote?

INGREDIENTS

4 ripe red plums, halved
225 g / 8 oz / 2 cups strawberries, halved
225 g / 8 oz / 1¾ cups raspberries
30 ml / 2 tbsp light muscovado sugar
30 ml / 2 tbsp cold water
1 cinnamon stick
3 pieces of star anise
6 cloves
natural yogurt or fromage frais, to serve

Serves 4

1

Place all the ingredients, except the yogurt or fromage frais, in a heavy-based pan. Heat gently, without boiling, until the sugar dissolves and the fruit juices run.

2

Cover the pan and leave the fruit to infuse over a very low heat for about 5 minutes. Remove the spices from the compote before serving warm with natural yogurt or fromage frais.

Rhubarb Spiral Cobbler

Typical farmhouse fare: stewed rhubarb with spiral scone topping.

INGREDIENTS

675 g / 1½ lb rhubarb, sliced
45 ml / 3 tbsp orange juice
75 g / 3 oz / 6 tbsp caster sugar
200 g / 7 oz / 1¾ cups self-raising flour
250 ml / 8 fl oz / 1 cup natural yogurt
grated rind of 1 medium orange
30 ml / 2 tbsp demerara sugar
5 ml / 1 tsp ground ginger
Greek-style yogurt or custard, to serve

Serves 4

1

Preheat the oven to 200°C / 400°F / Gas Mark 6. Cook the rhubarb with the orange juice and two-thirds of the sugar until tender. Transfer to an ovenproof dish.

2

To make the topping, mix the flour with the remaining caster sugar, then gradually stir in enough of the yogurt to bind to a soft dough.

3

Roll out the dough on a floured surface to a 25 cm / 10 in square. Mix the orange rind, demerara sugar and ginger, then sprinkle this over the dough.

4

Roll up the dough quite tightly, then cut into about 10 slices. Arrange the dough slices over the rhubarb.

5

Bake the cobbler for 15–20 minutes, or until the spirals are well risen and golden brown. Serve warm with Greek-style yogurt or custard.

BAKING

Dark Fruit Cake

With its colourful citrus and candied fruit topping, this tasty cake needs no further decoration.

INGREDIENTS

175 g / 6 oz / 1 cup currants
175 g / 6 oz / 1 cup raisins
115 g / 4 oz / ²⁄₃ cup sultanas
50 g / 2 oz / ¼ cup glacé cherries, halved
45 ml / 3 tbsp Madeira or sherry
175 g / 6 oz / ¾ cup butter
175 g / 6 oz / 1 cup dark brown sugar
2 extra large eggs
200 g / 7 oz / 1¾ cups plain flour
10 ml / 2 tsp baking powder
10 ml / 2 tsp each ground ginger,
allspice and cinnamon
15 ml / 1 tbsp molasses
15 ml / 1 tbsp milk
25 g / 1 oz / ¼ cup glacé fruit, chopped
115 g / 4 oz / 1 cup walnuts or pecan
nuts, chopped

For the decoration
225 g / 8 oz / 1 cup granulated sugar
120 ml / 4 fl oz / ½ cup water
1 lemon, thinly sliced
½ orange, thinly sliced
150 g / 5 oz / ½ cup orange marmalade
glacé cherries

Serves 12

1

Mix the currants, raisins, sultanas and cherries in a bowl. Stir in the Madeira or sherry. Cover and leave overnight.

2

Preheat the oven to 150°C / 300°F / Gas Mark 2. Line and grease a 23 cm / 9 in round springform tin. Cream the butter and sugar in a mixing bowl until light and fluffy. Beat in the eggs, one at a time.

3

Sift the flour, baking powder and spices together. Fold into the butter mixture in batches. Fold in the molasses, milk, dried fruit and liquid, glacé fruit and nuts.

4

Spoon into the tin, spreading out so there is a slight hollow in the centre of the mixture.
Bake for 2½–3 hours, until a skewer inserted in the cake comes out clean. Cover with foil when the top is golden to prevent over-browning. Cool in the tin on a rack.

5

Mix the sugar and water in a saucepan and bring to the boil. Add the citrus slices and cook for 20 minutes. Remove the fruit with a slotted spoon. Pour the remaining syrup over the cake and leave to cool. Melt the marmalade, then brush over the top of the cake. Decorate with the candied fruit and glacé cherries.

Cranberry Muffins

A tea or breakfast dish that is not too sweet.

INGREDIENTS

350 g / 12 oz / 3 cups plain flour
15 ml / 1 tsp baking powder
pinch of salt
115 g / 4 oz / ½ cup caster sugar
2 eggs
150 ml / ¼ pint / ⅔ cup milk
50 ml / 2 fl oz / 4 tbsp corn oil
freshly grated rind of 1 orange
150 g / 5 oz cranberries

Makes 12

1

Preheat the oven to 190°C / 375°F / Gas Mark 5. Line 12 deep muffin tins with paper cases. Mix the flour, baking powder, salt and caster sugar together.

2

Lightly beat the eggs with the milk and oil. Add them to the dry ingredients and blend to make a smooth batter. Stir in the orange rind and cranberries. Divide the mixture between the muffin cases and bake for 25 minutes until risen and golden. Leave to cool in the tins for a few minutes, and serve warm or cold.

Scotch Pancakes

Serve these while still warm, with butter and jam.

INGREDIENTS

225 g / 8 oz / 2 cups self-raising flour
50 g / 2 oz / 4 tbsp caster sugar
50 g / 2 oz / 4 tbsp butter, melted
1 egg
300 ml / ½ pint / 1¼ cups milk
15 g / ½ oz / 1 tbsp hard white fat

Makes 24

1

Mix the flour and sugar together. Add the melted butter and egg with two-thirds of the milk. Mix to a smooth batter – it should be thin enough to find its own level.

2

Heat a griddle or a heavy-based frying pan and wipe it with a little hard white fat. When hot, drop spoonfuls of the mixture on to the hot griddle or pan. When bubbles come to the surface of the pancakes, flip them over to cook until golden on the other side. Keep the pancakes warm wrapped in a dish towel while cooking the rest of the mixture.

Harvest Loaf

The centrepiece for celebrations when the harvest is safely gathered in, the harvest loaf is a potent symbol of country life. It is too salty to eat, but looks wonderful. It is traditionally displayed at the altar amongst the fruit and vegetables and other offerings from the people of the parish. Although there were many different designs of harvest loaf, the most enduringly popular was the wheatsheaf, symbolic as it is of the harvest and the vital importance of bread as "the staff of life".

INGREDIENTS

1.5kg / 3½ lb / 14 cups strong white flour
30 ml / 2 tbsp salt
2 x 10g / ¼ oz sachets easy-blend dried yeast
750–900 ml / 1¼–1½ pints / 3–3¾ cups hand-hot water
beaten eggs, to glaze

Makes 2 x 800g / 1¾ lb loaves

1

Sift the flour and salt into a large mixing bowl and stir in the yeast. Add enough hand-hot water to make a rough dough. Knead on a lightly floured surface for about 10 minutes, until smooth and elastic. Place the dough in a lightly oiled bowl, cover and leave to prove for 1–2 hours, until it has doubled in bulk.

2

Preheat the oven to 220°C / 425°F / Gas Mark 7. Oil and flour a large baking sheet. Roll out about 225 g / 8 oz of the dough into a 30 cm / 12 in long cylinder. Place it on the baking sheet and flatten slightly with your hand. This will form the body of the bread, symbolizing the long stalks of the wheatsheaf. The high salt content in the dough makes it easier to work, but the bread is more decorative than palatable.

3

Roll and shape about 350 g / 12 oz of the remaining dough into a crescent; place this at the top of the cylinder and flatten. Divide the remaining dough in half. Take one half and divide it in two again. Use one half to make the stalks of the wheat by rolling into narrow ropes and placing on the "stalk" of the sheaf. Use the other half to make a plait to decorate the finished loaf where the stalks meet the ears of wheat.

4

Use the remaining dough to make the ears of wheat. Roll it into small sausage shapes and snip each a few times with scissors to give the effect of the separate ears. Place these on the crescent shape, fanning out from the base until the wheatsheaf is complete. Position the plait between the stalks and the ears of wheat. Brush the wheatsheaf with the beaten egg. Bake for 20 minutes, then reduce the heat to 160°C / 325°F / Gas Mark 3 and bake for 20 minutes more.

Potato Bread

Mashed potatoes make a lovely loaf. Ensure the liquid is only hand-hot when added.

INGREDIENTS

*225 g / 8 oz potatoes, peeled and
halved or quartered
30 ml / 2 tbsp vegetable oil
250 ml / 8 fl oz / 1 cup lukewarm milk
675 g / 1½ lb / 6 cups strong white flour
15 ml / 1 tbsp salt
20 ml / 4 tsp easy-blend dried yeast*

Makes 2 loaves

1

Cook the potatoes in a saucepan of salted
water for 20–30 minutes. Drain and reserve
the cooking water. Return the potatoes to
the pan and mash with oil and milk. Mix
the flour, salt and yeast together. Put the
potato mixture in a bowl. Stir in
250 ml / 8 fl oz / 1 cup of the potato
cooking water, then gradually stir in the
flour mixture to form a stiff dough.

2

Knead the dough for 10 minutes. Grease two
23 x 13 cm / 9 x 5 in loaf tins. Roll the
dough into 20 small balls. Place two rows of
balls in each pan. Cover with clear film and
leave in a warm place to rise. Preheat the
oven to 200°C / 400°F / Gas Mark 6. Bake
the loaves for 10 minutes, then lower the
heat to 190°C / 375°F / Gas Mark 5 and
bake for about 40 minutes more.

Irish Soda Bread

This traditional farmhouse loaf needs no rising, so is perfect for unexpected guests.

INGREDIENTS

*225 g / 8 oz / 2 cups plain white
flour, plus extra for dusting
115 g / 4 oz / 1 cup wholemeal flour
5 ml / 1 tsp bicarbonate of soda
5 ml / 1 tsp salt
25 g / 1 oz / 2 tbsp butter, softened
300 ml / ½ pint / 1¼ cups buttermilk*

Makes 1 loaf

1

Preheat the oven to 200°C / 400°F / Gas
Mark 6. Grease a baking sheet. Sift the dry
ingredients into a bowl. Make a well in the
centre and add the butter and buttermilk.
Gradually incorporate the surrounding flour
to make a soft dough. Gather the dough
into a ball. Knead the dough on a floured
surface for 3 minutes. Shape into a round.

2

Place the round on the baking sheet. Cut a
cross in the top with a sharp knife. Dust with
flour, then bake for 40–50 minutes or until
golden brown. Transfer to a rack to cool.

PRESERVES

Windfall Pear Chutney

The apparently unusable bullet-hard pears that litter the ground underneath
old pear trees after high winds are ideal for this tasty chutney.

INGREDIENTS

675 g / 1½ lb pears, peeled and cored
3 onions, chopped
175 g / 6 oz / 1 cup raisins
1 cooking apple, cored and chopped
50 g / 2 oz / ⅓ cup preserved stem ginger
115 g / 4 oz / 1 cup walnuts, chopped
1 garlic clove, chopped
grated rind and juice of 1 lemon
600 ml / 1 pint / 2½ cups cider vinegar
175 g / 6 oz / 1 cup soft brown sugar
2 cloves
5 ml / 1 tsp salt

Makes about 2 kg / 4½ lb

1

Chop the pears roughly and put them in a bowl. Add the onions, raisins, apple, ginger, walnuts and garlic, with the lemon juice and rind. Put the vinegar, sugar, cloves and salt into a saucepan. Gently heat, stirring until the sugar has dissolved, then bring to the boil briefly and pour over the fruit. Cover and leave overnight.

2

Tip the mixture into a preserving pan and boil gently for 1½ hours until soft. Spoon into warm, sterilized jars. Seal with a waxed disc and cover with a cellophane top.

Dill Pickle

Dill is easy to grow and is a delightful herb. It goes well with fish and gives a superb flavour to this popular pickle.

INGREDIENTS

6 small cucumbers
475 ml / 16 fl oz / 2 cups water
1 litre / 1¾ pints / 4 cups white wine vinegar
115 g / 4 oz / ½ cup salt
3 bay leaves
45 ml / 3 tbsp dill seed
2 garlic cloves, slivered

Makes about 2.5 litres / 4 pints / 10 cups

1

Slice the cucumbers into medium-thick slices. Put the water, vinegar and salt in a saucepan. Bring to the boil, then immediately remove from the heat.

2

Layer the herbs and garlic between slices of cucumber in sterilized preserving jars until the jars are full, then cover with the warm salt and vinegar mixture. When the liquid is cold, close the jars. Leave on a sunny windowsill for at least 1 week before using.

Rhubarb and Ginger Mint Jam

Ginger mint is easily grown in the garden, and is just the thing to boost the flavour of rhubarb jam.

INGREDIENTS

2 kg / 4½ lb rhubarb
250 ml / 8 fl oz / 1 cup water
juice of 1 lemon
5 cm / 2 in piece of fresh root ginger,
1.4 kg / 3 lb / 6 cups granulated sugar
115 g / 4 oz / ⅔ cup preserved stem
ginger, chopped
30–45 ml / 2–3 tbsp fresh ginger
mint leaves, very finely chopped

Makes about 2.75 kg / 6 lb

NOTE

To confirm the setting point, spoon a little of the jam on to a cold saucer. Leave for 2 minutes. A skin should have formed on the jam which will wrinkle if you push it gently with your finger.

1

Cut the rhubarb into short lengths. Place the rhubarb, water and lemon juice in a preserving pan and bring to the boil. Peel and bruise the root ginger and add to the pan. Reduce the heat and simmer, stirring frequently, until the rhubarb is soft.

2

Remove the ginger. Add the sugar and stir until dissolved. Boil rapidly for 10–15 minutes, or until setting point is reached. Skim off scum from the surface of the jam, then add the stem ginger and the chopped ginger mint leaves. Pour into sterilized glass jars, seal with waxed paper discs and cover with tightly fitting cellophane tops.

Crab Apple Jelly

Crab apple trees are so pretty with abundant flowers and glowing red fruit, and though their role in the garden is mainly decorative, this jelly is a delicious way to make use of the fruit.

INGREDIENTS

preserving sugar (see method)
1 kg / 2¼ lb crab apples
3 cloves
water (see method)

**Makes about 1 kg / 2¼ lb from each
600 ml / 1 pint / 2½ cups liquid**

1

Preheat the oven to 120°C / 250°F / Gas Mark ½. Put the preserving sugar in a heatproof bowl and warm in the oven for 15 minutes. Wash the apples and cut them in half but do not peel or core. Place the apples and cloves in a large saucepan.

2

Pour in water to cover. Bring to the boil, reduce the heat and simmer until soft. Strain the mixture into a bowl. Measure the juice and add 450 g / 1 lb / 2 cups sugar for each 600 ml / 1 pint / 2½ cups of juice. Pour into a pan and heat gently. Stir until the sugar dissolves, then boil rapidly until the setting point is reached. Pour into warm, sterilized jars and seal.

Rosehip and Apple Jelly

*This recipe uses windfall apples and rosehips gathered from the hedgerows.
The jelly is rich in vitamin C as well as full of flavour.*

INGREDIENTS

*1 kg / 2¼ lb windfall apples, peeled,
trimmed and quartered*
450 g / 1 lb firm, ripe rosehips
300 ml / ½ pint / 1¼ cups boiling water
preserving sugar (see method)

**Makes about 1 kg / 2¼ lb from each
600 ml / 1 pint / 2½ cups liquid**

OPPOSITE: *Fruit jellies allow you to savour the taste of summer even during the winter months.*

1

Place the quartered apples in a preserving pan with just enough water to cover them. Bring to the boil and cook until the apples are pulpy. Meanwhile, chop the rosehips coarsely in a food processor. Add the rosehips to the cooked apples with the boiling water. Leave to simmer for 10 minutes, then remove from the heat and allow to stand for 10 minutes more. Pour the mixture into a thick jelly bag suspended over a bowl and leave to strain overnight.

2

Preheat the oven to 120°C / 250°F / Gas Mark ½. Measure the juice and allow 400 g / 14 oz / 1¾ cups preserving sugar for each 600 ml / 1 pint / 2½ cups of liquid. Warm the sugar in the oven. Pour the juice into a pan and bring to the boil, stir in the warmed sugar until it has dissolved completely, then leave to boil until a setting point is reached. Finally, pour the jelly into warm, sterilized jars and seal securely.

Index